The story of the Reebok Stadium - Foreword

Gordon Hargreaves
Chairman BWFC

Gordon Hargreaves,
Chairman, Bolton Wanderers Football Club

At 1.30 pm on Saturday January 10th 1998 Deputy Prime Minister John Prescott unveiled a plaque to officially open The Reebok Stadium.

It was the final action in an eleven year journey which has taken Bolton Wanderers out of its traditional Burnden Park home and into the most modern, up-to-date and expensive new stadium in Britain.

During those eleven years the whole face of the football club has changed beyond recognition. In 1987 we were starting our first ever season in the fourth division of the Football League. It was the culmination of seven years of declining fortune but Robbie Savage's goal 22 minutes from the end of our final game of the season at Wrexham ensured it was a one season experience and one we hope never to see repeated.

Today, just short of eleven years later, the club finds itself up among the elite of English soccer in the best League in the world, playing in the finest new stadium in the country and with a stock market listing.

The need for us to make the journey to The Reebok Stadium became apparent when, following the final report of Lord Justice Taylor, independent surveys confirmed that it was not possible to continue at Burnden Park on a satisfactory operational basis. In order to achieve our aims for the club and its supporters we had to move to a new home. Following up on professional advice we came to the conclusion that the 200 acre site at Lostock was the only feasible location out of 14 sites which were examined.

Work on the stadium eventually got underway in November of 1995 when the first turf was cut by the then Mayor of Bolton, Councillor Alan Rushton and Wanderers' President Nat Lofthouse OBE.

Bolton's President Nat Lofthouse OBE, Chairman, Gordon Hargreaves and the then Mayor of Bolton, Councillor Alan Rushton start the digging at the Middlebrook site, in November 1995.

Since that day we have suffered heartbreak and triumph both on and off the pitch, but by teamwork and co-operation between all parties involved during those eleven years, we have made a successful transition. It has been a massive project. I would imagine most of us have experienced a domestic house move and all the upheaval that entails. Multiply that a thousand-fold and you begin to get some idea of the scale of the move from Burnden to the Reebok. But the substantial benefits to the local community far outweighed the headaches. Over 3,000 new jobs have been created at the Middlebrook Development, adjoining the Reebok Stadium. Similarly, our stadium and proposed associated leisure and sports facilities, which will be completed around the turn of the century will provide many more new employment opportunities, as well as the very best for spectators and participants alike.

The public road network around the stadium site has been improved out of all recognition.

Within the pages of this book is contained the story of how a vision was turned into a reality. It is also the story of how sport, business and government can work together in harmony for the benefit of the community as a whole.

I hope you enjoy reading it.

Gordon Hargreaves, Chairman, BWFC

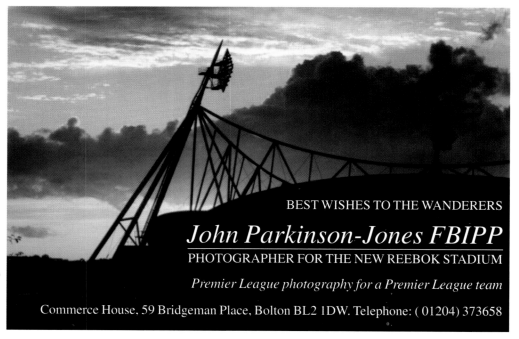

Contents

With grateful thanks to all contributors, especially:-
Bolton Evening News; Chris Tofalus Photography; John Parkinson-Jones Photographer; Liam O'Connor; Brian White;
Reebok UK; Sucha Design; Touchline T.V.; Damien James. Ian Lawson Photography; Stuart Clarke Photography
Compiled by Paul Fletcher, Chief Executive, Reebok Stadium
Designed by Mike Trevena, Atom Design Associates.
Published by Arrow Publishing, Lytham St Annes, Lancashire
Front Cover Photography by kind permission of Ian Lawson

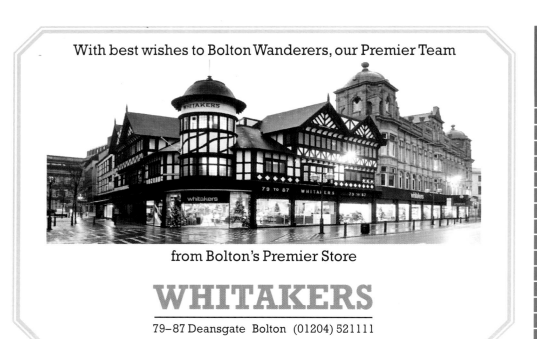

The Challenge, Leaving Burnden Park

Graham Ball, F.R.I.C.S.
Project Director BWFC

Bolton Wanderers Football Club has been an important part of the local community for over 100 years, and the history and achievements of the Football Club have been acknowledged nationally, during this period whilst the Wanderers played at Burnden Park, Bolton. Unfortunately, time would not stand still for the Club nor the local community and, in reality, Burnden Park was decaying whilst unfortunately at the same time, a large proportion of the Club's fans were becoming part of the local unemployment situation.

Although discussions regarding relocation took place as early as 1986, more serious discussions began in the early 1990's. The Football Club and Bolton Council decided to try and harness the power of both bodies to improve the overall local situation. The Club was anxious to rebuild the decaying stadium by way of providing a facility for their fans that could be the best in Europe for its size. Large tracts of industrial land that had been available and unused for generations, started to look very promising.

The requirements of the Council were for a stadium that was an architectural statement, and also incorporated extensive community facilities and benefits on non-football occasions. The requirements of the Football Club were for a stadium that offered new horizons in spectator safety and comforts, but which would equally serve the community for the other 340 days per year, to subsidise in part the costs of the stadium but, additionally, for the stadium to be the centre of community sporting opportunities which would be created in the adjoining and surrounding areas.

The continuing endeavours of the Football Club and the Council, along with the Partner chosen by the Council to develop the non-football/sports areas, have resulted in the attractive development, known as Middlebrook, Horwich, Bolton. Middlebrook occupies some 200 acres, adjoining the former run-down areas, and convenient for the nearby motorway system. Infrastructure for the site has been completed, at a cost of some £14m, which includes improvements to Junction 6/M61 motorway, and six other local off-site road junctions, as well as starter industrial units for employment and landscaping proposals.

In supporting the Middlebrook Project, the Football Club has taken the lead in the creation of a pedestrian footbridge, over a busy access road, and is obtaining anticipated assistance from football sources towards the construction of a new Rail Halt on the adjoining main line.

An indoor/outdoor Tennis Centre, to be run on a community basis as opposed to membership usage, is to be constructed, along with a full size running track and quality football pitch for the Council's schoolboy town team, etc. Further planned intentions are for a full Football and Sports Academy on adjoining lands, extending to over 100 acres of greenfield facilities on a regional user basis.

Importantly, during the official opening ceremony of the Reebok Stadium (10th January 1998) it was announced that 2,850 new jobs had already been created at Middlebrook and forecast that overall 4,000 new jobs should be created by the year 2000.

The Stadium

The Club decided to maximise spectator comfort and community benefits, concentrating on quality rather than quantity of spectator seats.

Many other stadia were studied, both in the UK and in Europe, in order to seek out the best in design for the new Stadium, which would meet the latest FIFA and UEFA requirements. Over 2,750 car parking spaces have been incorporated with the design, suitably segregated between home and visiting supporters.

Wider than normal terrace units give unrivalled comfort and leg room for 25,000 spectators, accommodated in the lower and upper tiers. The sweeping curves of the upper tier means no one is ever seated more than 90 metres from the centre of the field. Each of the 8 spectator concourses has two concession units selling a variety of foods, all able to be consumed in view of one of the play-back TV screens in operation all around the Stadium. Spectator comfort, multi-usage, and quality of finishes are the key to the Stadium's success.

Arriving at the Stadium, a double height Reception Foyer gives the instant feel of a Five Star Hotel. Two lifts, finished in polished walnut, take guests up to the first, second and third floors, where various corporate executive areas cater for up to 2,050 people on match days. The design and finishes within all the various corporate facilities are like no other stadium, certainly in Europe, and most probably the world. The Stadium boasts 46 executive box suites, available on non-match days for business use. Two function suites, one holding 400 and the other holding 600, give Bolton one of the North West's premier business conference facilities.

Community commitments are further provided by an Exhibition Hall, some 35,000 sq. ft. in size, in the main East Stand structure. This Hall can be used for exhibitions, concerts, conferences and banquets, and doubles up as a community sports hall.

Perfection does not come cheaply, but the overall cost of £35m. (£1,250 per seat approx.) offers good value to the fans and the community for the next 100 years.

Burnden Park has served us all well. It will remain a golden memory for myself and many thousands of people in Bolton and throughout the country. Sadly it could not keep up with the club's ambitions. Burnden Park will remain forever linked with Bolton Wanderers' rich history, but the Reebok will allow us to take part in a new century of football in magnificent surroundings.

B.W.F.C has been an important part of the local community for over 100 years

The Pitch -

Richard Norton,
Groundsman, BWFC

The Pitch

Levelling work under progress.

The £400,000 investment in underground heating has already disappeared from view.

The modern football stadium with its high stands and enclosed space presents an alien environment for the cultivation and management of the humble grass plant. Today's football pitch is no longer a bit of green turf in summer and brown mud in winter, the demands of the game and TV coverage have led to a comprehensive re-evaluation of surface quality and consequently construction methods and subsequent management techniques.

Bolton Wanderers recognised at an early stage that the playing surface for the new Stadium would be a vital component in the development. Some of the best brains in modern sports turf culture were consulted during the design period. Pitch design was led by Professional Sportsturf Design (PSD) and complemented by J. Mallinson (Ormskirk) Ltd, the Sportsground contractors and the Sportsturf Research Institute (STRI).

- Laser installed levels.
- Engineered Sand, Soil rootzone growing medium, of uniform composition
- Automatic sprinkler system - vital to ensure maximum growth potential during the important summer months.
- Uniform substructure incorporating piped drainage system
- Hot water undersoil heating system
- Latest grass cultivars including Barcampsia a tufted hair-grass with improved tolerance of shade conditions.
- Rootzone stabilisation with the incorporation of 'polythene' filaments (via fibresand) into the upper rootzone element.

Blake makes the most of the new surface.
Photograph Bolton Evening News.

Early groundwork in Winter 1995.

The Reebok pitch embraces these modern methods, in effect the playing surface is a combination of soil science, engineering, botany, horticulture and groundmanship. Good turfgrass is influenced by two major factors - climate and soil, the latter can be controlled via construction and groundmanship, but unfortunately, the British climate is not so easily restrained.

Bolton's new pitch comprises the following features, which are typical in today's constructions.

After the official sod cutting ceremony in November, 1995 the initial enablement works contract started in earnest in January, 1996. Following this, the Pitch Contractor J. Mallinson (Ormskirk) Ltd established his construction team on site in February and commenced operations by installing the drainage system.

Work continued on a steady basis apart from a couple of difficulties with adverse weather and problems with sourcing the temporary water and power supplies for the irrigation system. It now seems a long time ago that the pitch took shape in the midst of rough marshy ground at the end of Green Pine Road in Horwich.

Sowing down took place on schedule at the end of May, 1996 rapidly followed by the erection of a perimeter fence to keep out unwanted guests. Although on a couple of occasions some more determined visitors were able to scale the fence and leave initials of competitor clubs as evidence of their visit.

Establishment of the new grass was steady rather than spectacular and continued as the magnificent new Stadium was constructed around the outside.

Odd headaches arose from time to time because of fungal disease (young grass is particularly susceptible to attack) which could not be treated immediately because of access restraints caused by huge cranes erecting the structural steelwork and the like.

In the weeks running up to the first game, myself and the football club became actively involved in the day to day regime. Work was then concentrated on finalising the permanent irrigation set up, maximising the grass growth and root development, repairing incursions from the Stadium builders and installing the goalposts.

The pitch has now been used for a number of games and training sessions and received favourable comments from the playing staff. The intention was to build a firm, smooth and fast playing surface and to date the performance seems to match the intention.

The only cloud on the horizon remains the inevitable winter shade pattern at the pitch surface, which as expected does affect the southern end of the ground. However, work will continue with experimentation using different grass cultivars and hopefully we will one day develop a grass plant that will tolerate having its head kicked off in the dark.

The first step on a £35 million journey.

A temporary fence around the pitch.

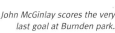

Des McBain
Chief Executive, BWFC

The Last Match at Burnden Park . . .

John McGinlay scores the very last goal at Burnden park.

It is 8.30 am on Friday 25th April 1997 the day of the last Football League match scheduled to be played on Burnden Park, the home of Bolton Wanderers for the past 102 years and for me for almost the last 20 of those years.

All tickets for the capacity of 22,000 had been sold for many weeks.

Appreciating the significance of the occasion, Charlton Athletic had waived their rights to their full allocation of tickets and only taken 250 seats which had ensured that the Embankment was again being used by Bolton supporters, many of whom had made a special request to stand in the area they had spent so many emotional years watching their team.

In less than 12 hours the whistle would blow for the kick off and 2 hours later the gates would finally close on an incredible piece of English footballing history as one of the founder members of the Football League closed its gates for the last time at the old stadium.

For the last time a pre-match walk down the players tunnel onto the pitch to discuss with the Head Groundsman, Richard Norton, the state of the playing area which had given rise to so many concerns over the years as to its playability, a meeting with Maintenance Foreman, Roy Crompton, over the condition of the stadium which was now looking oh so tired and finally a discussion with the Safety Officer, Colin Sumner, on the safety and security aspects which are part and parcel of each match.

Today, however, was not quite like any other match. It was unique.

Many, many hours had been spent with the Local Authority and the Police discussing the final match in an attempt to ensure that everything went smoothly and that there were no problems or injuries.

Only time would tell.

The Board of Directors had discussed in detail how to commemorate the closure. It was originally to be extremely low key as it was a concern for Colin Todd that the players may be distracted by the occasion from the prime target of promotion. As the day had drawn nearer, the Club had reached its first goal of promotion and finally the Championship.

The celebrations and reflections could now take place with no inhibitions. 10 am and SKY TV technicians were by now in full swing preparing for the live screening of this historic event.

The Administration Department and Ticket Office were still having to disappoint hundreds of supporters wishing to attend the game and not able to obtain tickets.

By lunch time match day staff were arriving some five hours before necessary in order to soak up the atmosphere for the last time.

4 pm and the first invited guests of the Club were assembling at two hotels in the town to partake of a pre match buffet before attending the game. There had been no way that the facilities at Burnden Park could have been improved without major financial outlay and certainly not for the number of ex-players and guests who wished to pay their respects to a fine "Old Lady".

6 pm and at last the turnstiles were open and supporters were able to either meet with the friends they had stood or sat next to for so many years or greet the players as they approached the players entrance for the last time. By 7 pm the Guests had arrived at the ground and the ex-Players of the past were ready to parade around the pitch led by the Club President, Nat Lofthouse.

The Stadium was buzzing by 7.30 pm with virtually everyone inside soaking up the unique atmosphere.

The Referee blew his whistle for kick off and the final match was under way. Although not yet able to relax, attention was now focused on the game. Charlton scored the first goal. Were they going to spoil the occasion. No way. A final result of Bolton Wanderers 4, Charlton Athletic 1, ensured that Burnden Park would go out with a bang. A fairy tale ending also for John McGinlay who scored the last ever goal at Burnden Park.

A lap of honour following a 4-1 victory. Photographs Bolton Evening News.

Immediately after the match the centre spot was ceremoniously removed by the Chairman followed by unforgettable scenes from an emotional 22,000 crowd who were allowed to stay as long as they wished to pay their last respects.

The referee's whistle and linesmen's flags were presented to the club after the match for the club's museum.

With the SKY TV technicians removing their cabling it looked as though the demolition of the famous old stadium had already begun.

11.30 pm and it was now time for the staff and services to stand down on this special night. A few tears were mixed in with the waste paper on the terraces.

One last look back down the tunnel as the floodlights were extinguished for the last time.

It was the end of a special era.

The rest is HISTORY.

Fans on the terraces for the very last time at Burnden Park.

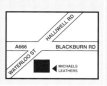
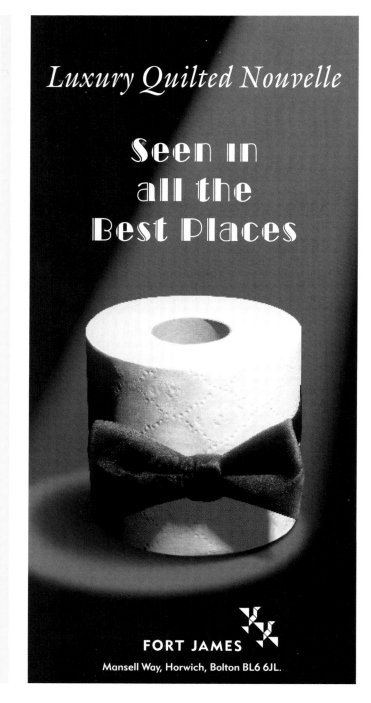

The Past and the Future

Nat Lofthouse O.B.E.
President BWFC

Nat receives football's greatest trophy, F.A.cup 1958.

It seems like only yesterday I walked into Burnden Park for the very first time as a keen young would - be professional footballer hoping to make the grade.

I did not know then that I would go on to make 503 appearances; score 285 goals; win 33 England International caps scoring 30 goals; and, become an O.B.E. Doesn't time pass quickly?

It was 1939 when I first fell in love with Bolton Wanderers and I was 14 years old. I have been employed by Bolton Wanderers Football Club for nearly 60 years and loved every minute. But I never thought, in those early days we would ever leave Burnden Park especially the day I made my debut as a young 15 year old.

Nat Lofthouse scores another goal for the "Trotters" in the 1958 F.A. cup.

Major changes started to come into the game starting in the early 1970's. When I first began my career the manager was also the secretary and rarely came onto the training fields even though he picked the team every week. It was someone else's job to get the players fit. The 1970's saw the profile of the football manager change from backroom staff to star status. Today's football sees the managers often more valuable than the players!

The 1970's saw another major change quietly come into football. The ball itself. The modern plastic coated ball would stay the same consistently throughout the game irrespective of the weather. This benefit would have saved me many headaches in the 1940's and 1950's when a mistimed header, at 4.35pm in mid November, with the lace coming undone, could cause stars, bells and a thumping headache all weekend.

The new ball has quickened up the game and brought in more entertainment. I think it was in the 1950's when I saw the Brazilian's curve the ball around a defensive wall. They did not have our winters to contend with. Now our British players can match the continentals at most of the ball dribbling and shooting skills.

The second major noticeable change has arrived in the last decade, the pitch.

It was unbelievable to see the pitch being laid for the new Reebok Stadium in 1995, twelve months before they began to build the Stadium! I would pop up each week to watch lorryloads of gravel, stone and sand being laid and kept wondering when the soil and grass seed would arrive. Wrong again. The new pitches are laid on 70% sand with only a small amount of soil. I am told that this allows the water to drain through very easily. I wish they had known that at the Baseball Ground, Derby in the 1960's, I am sure my goal tally would have been much higher.

When I first heard the news that we would be leaving Burnden Park, I must admit I was against the idea. But as I sat and thought about the changes I had seen in my time I slowly realised it would be the best option for Bolton Wanderers in the long run.

The Premier League has proved a great success and it is the only place for Bolton Wanderers. We could not have achieved a regular place in the Premier League at Burnden Park because now we need to compete with other teams with our off the field activities as well as try to win games on the field.

At the new Reebok we have many hundreds of visitors looking around the place, many on guided tours and I am always pleased to pop out of my office to say hello when I can. The most popular question is 'How would I like to be playing in today's football' my answer is always the same 'definitely not'. I had a wonderful time during my career in the greatest era, in the greatest team, in the greatest town. It is now someone else's turn, and my turn to sit and watch.

The fact that I can watch my hometown Club in a beautifully cushioned seat in one of the finest Stadiums in the world makes me very proud. The past has been great, who's to say the future will not be even better.

Nat Lofthouse O.B.E.

Nat Lofthouse

S e p t e m b e r

G r o u n d w o r k

Introduction

Damien James, BSc(Hons), ARICS, Quantity Surveyor, Birse Construction.

Early piling work begins.

For those of us at Birse Construction who were fortunate enough to be selected to work on the Reebok Stadium few could have realised the size and the magnitude of the task ahead. Of course the staff knew it would not be the same as any other project that they had known but their achievements come 1st September 1997 were to be acknowledged by thousands of Wanderers fans.

For in the twelve months prior to that momentous occasion, there was another team playing at the Reebok Stadium. That team was the construction team, which assembled like an elite premiership force,combined the subtle nuances of its own midfield tacticians, fluent silky skills of its wing players,the driving force at its helm and ultimately the dynamic ability and innovation to produce the goods when it counted. On its day this team of 35 assembled from all corners of the northwest and beyond, could be held in the same esteem as its famous predecessors at the Colisseum of Rome.

The effect of working on such a project could be measured in terms of experience and curriculum vitae, however in being part of history in the making we all know what we have gained.

The new season was already underway and with it Bolton Wanderers march to a triumphant First Division Championship. Burnden Park continued to house its faithful supporters during its Nationwide challenge. The last season for this famous football ground would not be forgotten by its replacement with the new Stadium at Horwich.

On site progress was good, although hindered by the incessant raincloud that had descended and remained stationary over Middlebrook. This stage of the consruction concentrated on the formation of concrete bases on which to place the huge steel frame that was currently being fabricated by Watsons. For those who regard construction as being a source of adventure, it is this stage in the project that makes you grateful that the labourers and tradesmen do get the opportunity in the summer to enjoy some good weather.

The conditions on site had not reached the low that they were to, but the status of the existing ground was deteriorating under the continuity of the rainfall.

It was essential to maintain progress in line with our commitments and every effort was being made at this stage so as not to jeopardise our obligations.

In a television interview, Bruce Rioch payed tribute to his former Board and extended the praise of them being the best board he had ever worked with. In a day and age where football could be measured in terms of economic growth and personal prosperity, compliments like these are few and far between when ex managers talk about their former employers.

Having aspired to gaining a little bit of inside knowledge and with it an understanding that football can still evolve from its grass roots, I can understand the significance of Bruce Rioch's statement. Many advocate that the construction industry houses an adversarial approach which ultimately leads to confrontation between the parties. For some and probably quite considerable in number (if you were to consider the money that the legal profession earns from construction industry disputes) the prospect of confrontation and egotistical exposure holds the key to their involvement in the construction industry. We as a construction team would never deny that our twelve months saw us engage in some unsavoury incidents on the field of play, which like the footballing analogy that I am drawing were no more than signs of petulance and an opportunity to flex muscles.

All things considered, the key relationship on the project was that between Birse Construction and Bolton Wanderers Football Club, suffice to say, if there was anyone who doubted the credence of Bruce Rioch's words, I can find at least 35 people who will be willing to make you reconsider. The involvement in such a project was enhanced by the willingness to openly engage in the activities of the construction team. The Bolton Wanderers team provided the touchline support that every team on the pitch requires to be a success.

The achievement of constructing the Stadium in the allotted time span cannot be treated lightly, in an industry where most projects are judged by time, cost and quality, for one of the magnitude of The Reebok Stadium to achieve all three in fourteen months underlines the success of the construction team.

All construction photographs by kind permission of Chris Tofalos.

Sure we weren't supposed to be on the pitch but neither were the other twenty or so who were re-enacting a goalmouth incident.

In May 1996 the pitch had already been laid and was enclosed with palisade fencing. My first visit to the Stadium was with my dog late on a Tuesday evening that month and my intention was to photograph and encapsulate the current status of the then to be construction site. I think I managed to take two photographs before being asked by fully kitted Wanderers fans to take their picture in what they were guessing to be,the centre circle. Sure we weren't supposed to be on the pitch but neither were the other twenty or so who were re-enacting a goalmouth incident.

In June 1996 as the machines rolled onto the greenfield area of the site, the visits continued, some monthly, some weekly, but most daily. Of all the photographs published on the stadium I would wager that there are a few collectors items on the mantelpieces of Bolton.

In those early months as the site was brought to formation, many visitors queried the necessity for a stream to run through the West Stand concourse, their return visits saw the stream move further and further out of the stadium, and with it more and more of the surrounding embankment.

The summer months of July and August are notoriously good in the construction industry. The sun is out,well sometimes, (there was a point when it felt like it had rained solidly on Middlebrook), the days are long, and everyone gets a tan, (well not those of us who are stuck inside a tin hut with the sun beating down and not enough petty cash to buy a fan).

Thankfully, Horwich has The Bromilow, which provided the welcome reward at the end of many an arduous day. Unfortunately my own business acumen had taken a holiday at this point, for if I could have bought shares in this pub in July 1996, by the time September 1997 came, I would have been a wealthy man. The August that followed highlighted the pressure that was ahead. Progress was on schedule but what was left to achieve seemed many months and a lot of hard work away.

There would be a good few in the team who could identify their receeding, greying hairline, their well bitten nails, their suitcases under their eyes, along with their 'crows feet' and their emerging pot bellies as being the result of the twelve months that lay ahead, (plus those who could blame their pot bellies on The Bromilow).

The Writer

In construction terms life can easily get viewed in projects completed rather than in the years in which they took place. For myself 1996 and 1997 were 'The Reebok Stadium', with nearly two years of my life absorbed by the project.

My role with this project was that of senior quantity surveyor. As one of a team of 35 staff we built this stadium from the ground up and these following monthly sections charts both our progress and my personal recollections of an arduous yet very gratifying period of my life.

Piling rigs commence foundation works.

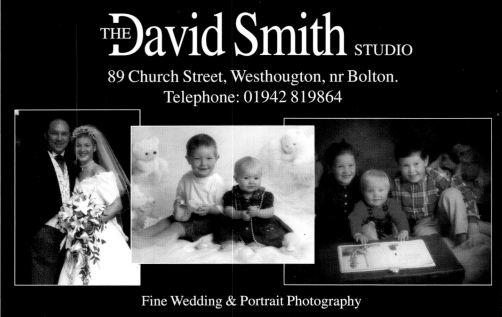

Simon Marland
Accountant & Historian BWFC

Bolton Wanderers

Burnden Park in 1997.

The Vicar of Christ Church Sunday School, Bolton, could have had little notion of the future of the acorn that he planted in 1874. His scholars and teachers formed an outdoor recreational club and the Reverend F.F. Wright was made its President.

In 1877 the Reverend objected to his club holding meetings in his school unless he was present. On 28th August that year the footballers amongst the club re-christened themselves Bolton Wanderers and established their headquarters in the more cheerful atmosphere of a hostelry.

They immediately began to take part in the move to popularise the game. Difficulties came aplenty, success and adversity came alike but the men of the early days carried Bolton Wanderers through.

The club was one of the twelve founder members of the Football League in 1888. Six years later they reached the FA Cup Final for the first time, losing to Notts County, and in 1895 left Pikes Lane and moved to Burnden Park.

Burnden Park became one of the most famous grounds in the country, hosting the 1901 FA Cup Final replay, a number of FA Cup semi finals, and saw a record crowd of 69,912 for a Bolton v Manchester City FA Cup tie in 1933. The ground also saw tragedy when in March 1946, 33 spectators lost their lives when a barrier collapsed.

Before the second World War Bolton Wanderers were second division champions in 1909, and won the FA Cup in 1923 (the first final played at Wembley), 1926 and 1929. The team of the 1920's is generally considered to be the greatest fielded by the club. Not only did they secure the Cup on three occasions they also finished third in the first division in 1921 and 1925.

During the 1930's the club slipped out of the top flight but returned in 1935 to put together a run of 29 consecutive years as members of the old first division.

Like other clubs, they were struck by a grievous blow by the second World War. The whole team joined up at the outbreak of hostilities and the captain, wing half Harry Goslin, lost his life in action in Italy.

Things gradually got back to normal and the club won the Football League North war cup in 1945 by defeating Manchester United over two legs. They followed this up with a victory over the Southern winners, Chelsea, at Stamford Bridge.

Loyal fans cheer on the "TROTTERS" in the 1958 F.A. cup run.

Wembley Stadium F.A. Cup 1923.

It was during this period that the club produced a great personality and one of England's greatest forwards in Nat Lofthouse. He went on to become the clubs record goalscorer with 285 first class goals. He also scored 30 goals in 33 England appearances, later becoming the Wanderers coach, manager and is now the club President.

The FA Cup brought the Wanderers to prominence in the 1950's. In 1953 they lost 4-3 to Blackpool when injuries in the final twenty minutes cost them the game. In 1958 the cup came back to Bolton when two Nat Lofthouse goals defeated Manchester United.

The sixties proved to be a difficult time for the club. Relegation was suffered from division one in 1964, they narrowly missed out on a quick return a season later and it was to be 1978 before the club got back into the top flight.

In 1971 the Wanderers suffered relegation to the third division for the first time but won the championship in 1973 to begin a climb back up the League ladder. After two near misses the club won the second division championship in 1978 but their stay in the top flight was to last for only two seasons.

Unfortunately, the slide couldn't be arrested and by 1987 the Wanderers found themselves in the basement of the Football League. The ten years that followed brought about the most exciting decade in the clubs history both on and off the park.

In 1988 promotion was won from the fourth division and a year later the club savoured a Wembley success in the Sherpa Van Trophy. In both 1990 and 1991 the club reached the third division play offs and in 1993 finally won promotion. In that same season the club gained national prominence by knocking Liverpool out of the FA Cup at Anfield.

In 1994 the Wanderers reached the FA Cup quarter finals for the first time since 1959. They did so by beating Premiership sides Everton and Arsenal on their own grounds and Aston Villa at Burnden Park.

The Premiership was reached in 1995 with an incredible 4-3 Wembley win over Reading in the play-off final. After just one season the club were relegated but bounced back at the first attempt.

1996/97 season proved to be the most successful League season in the clubs history as they won the first division championship. Club records tumbled. Most points in a season (98), most goals scored in a season (100) and most wins in a season (28).

It also proved to be the end of an era as the championship trophy was presented at the final Burnden Park game to make it a happy ending to 102 years at the ground.

The club kicked off the 1997/98 season back in the Premiership and at their new 25,000 all seater Reebok Stadium.

BOLTON COUNCIL
IS HELPING TO
MAKE THE BOROUGH A GREAT PLACE

TO LIVE, WORK, VISIT AND INVEST

The Water Place

BOLTON
METRO

BOLTON
Altogether Better

Bolton Metro Council - and Partners -

Des Grogan -
Secretarial Services,
Bolton Metro.

The idea of a Sports Village had been a dream of Bolton Council for a number of years and discussions had taken place with potential partners. These had proved fruitless.

However, when Bolton Wanderers were promoted in 1993 they faced the daunting task of improving Burnden Park or relocating to a new stadium, to meet the requirements of the Taylor Report, so it seemed natural that the two should get together.

Talks between the Club and the Council took place and the authority came up with the idea of Middlebrook as a possibility. Other areas were looked at but Middlebrook was the most attractive of all the sites.

The possibility of a partnership with the Wanderers fitted in with the plans. A major new stadium for football and other uses could form the centre piece for our ambitious proposal and attract the prestige and backing it required.

Then came the search for a developer who could help put the dream together.

The Emerson Group (including Orbit Developments) became interested and the proposals were enlarged to include more leisure, shopping, housing and business and office parks as well as the community sports and leisure facilities and the 25,000 seater stadium. The additional components would help finance the project and provide a greater variety to the site.

The business park is particularly important for the Council, providing opportunities for new and expanding businesses in the Borough. Following long and detailed discussions, Hitachi have been attracted to the site to develop a factory for new car components and the first phase will open in Spring 1998.

Substantial grants have been secured for the Middlebrook development including almost £5 million from the European Regional Development Fund towards infrastructure.

Together with Bolton Wanderers the authority is working on the development of the community sports and leisure facilities which will include indoor and outdoor tennis courts, health and fitness facilities, budget accommodation, a floodlit athletics track, a full-size football pitch, and multi-use games pitches.

A large grant from the Lawn Tennis Association for the indoor complex has already been won and a decision from the Lottery Board on some £9 million-plus of funding towards the project is awaited.

The new Reebok Stadium and the developments at Middlebrook have been the culmination of several years hard work by the Council, Bolton Wanderers, and Orbit Developments. Asda opened its doors in September, and were followed by other famous companies over the coming months including the Warner Brothers cinema in January 1998.

Middlebrook should be completed by the middle of 1999, providing work for over 3,000 people, housing, shopping, leisure and entertainment for the people of Bolton and the North West.

"The partnership between the Council, the Wanderers and Orbit have proved to be one of the most successful of its kind in the country and has brought much needed jobs and investment to the area," said Councillor Bob Howarth, Leader of the Council.

Orbit Developments kicks off at Middlebrook

Simon Wilson - Director of Orbit Developments.

Middlebrook is the North West's largest leisure and retail park, ideally located at junction 6 of the M61 motorway, adjacent to the Reebok Stadium. It is a joint venture development between Bolton Wanderers Football Club, Bolton Metropolitan Borough Council and Orbit Developments, the commercial division of the Emerson Group.

Formed in the late 1960's, Oribit Developments has become one of the largest privately-owned development and investment companies in the country.

In addition to providing extensive retail and leisure facilities alongside the new Reebok Stadium, Middlebrook will have a ten acre tennis centre developed in association with the Lawn Tennis Association, a business park offering 250,000 sq. ft of office space, a 14 acre residential housing area and a 500,000 sq. ft. industrial and warehousing development. The impact of all this on the local economy has been staggering with already almost 3,000 new jobs being created.

The leisure and retail facilities are amongst the finest in the country with a 12 screen Warner Village cinema, Hollywood Bowl and world renowned names such as McDonalds, Pizza Hut and KFC. Shopping at Middlebrook has over 3,000 car parking spaces serving retailers Asda, Allders at Home, Boots the Chemist, Furniture Workshop, Pets at Home, Texstyle World, Kingsbury Interiors, Scottish Power, Waldmans, Craft World, Carphone Warehouse, American Golf, Tog 24, Sports Division, JD Sports and JJB Sports.

Orbit Developments are also involved in a joint initiative with William Hargreaves Limited at The Valley in Bolton. The Valley is an integrated commercial, industrial and leisure development which lies within Bolton's City Challenge area.

The scheme consists of St. Peter's Office Park which will provide 250,000 sq. ft. of high quality office accommodation and Britannia Business Park which will offer some 450,000 sq. ft. of industrial and warehousing units in a variety of sizes.

Grant aid including regional selective assistance may be available to qualifying users. In addition, partners in the City Challenge Initiative - Bolton and Bury TEC, Bolton Metropolitan College and Bolton Institute of Higher Education - can provide bespoke training packages to companies.

The Reebok Stadium, Middlebrook centre and The Valley are a magnificent endorsement of the strength of Bolton's future in which Orbit Developments and the Emerson Group are proud to be involved.

Jones Homes - A Winner In Bolton!

The supporters of B.W.F.C. know all about tradition and success and since building its first residential development in Bolton some ten years ago these same qualities have enabled Jones Homes to become one of the areas most respected development companies.

A Tradition of Building Success

Jones Homes is the founder member of the Emerson Group, a privately owned property development company with its headquarters in Alderley Edge, Cheshire.

With 40 years experience it has established an enviable reputation for building award-winning homes of character and individuality in highly desirable locations, throughout the UK.

The hallmark of a Jones home is luxury accommodation coupled with high standards of construction, design and specification. The company's qualities have been recognised over the years by the National House Building Council in its 'Pride In The Job' schemes, the prestigious What House? Awards, the combined NHBC/DoE/RIBA Housing Design Awards and the Daily Mail/NHMB Green Leaf Awards.

Jones Homes offers its customers an unrivalled combination of service, quality, choice and value. Personal recommendation and repeat business are cornerstones of the company's success with families moving up over the years from one Jones home to another.

Nowhere is this more true than in Bolton where Jones Homes has enjoyed a long and happy relationship with the town and its residents.

'Premiership' Class in Bolton

Jones Homes earliest developments in Bolton date back to 1988. The company's first venture was Rydal Court, (Whitecroft Road), a new retirement homes development which was followed by Arundel Place, (also off Whitecroft Road).

Evidence that Bolton was to become an important location for Jones Homes came in 1990 when the new showhome opening weekend at Arundel Park (off Beaumont Road) attracted some 300 visitors!

Beaumont Chase (Wigan Road), Beaumont Rise (Hulton Lane), Sunninghill Park (St. Helen's Road) and Belmont Park (Wilkinson Road) are current developments where prospective home buyers have a choice from mews style to detached to suit all tastes and lifestyles.

Towards the end of 1998 Jones Homes will commence a new development at Middlebrook to provide 271 three and four bedroom semi-detached and detached homes. It will give the new workforce at the Middlebrook complex an opportunity to purchase top quality, value for money homes in an ideal location.

Living in a Jones home in Bolton means that families have the convenience of living close to the town's modern amenities while still enjoying the lovely open countryside of the West Pennine Moors. Showhomes are open every day from 10.00 am to 5.00 pm during the week and from 11.00 am to 5.00 pm at weekends.

So the message to house hunters looking for something special in Bolton is: "Come and join Bolton's other winning team!" For more information about Jones Homes in Bolton: call the Property Shop on 01625 588300.

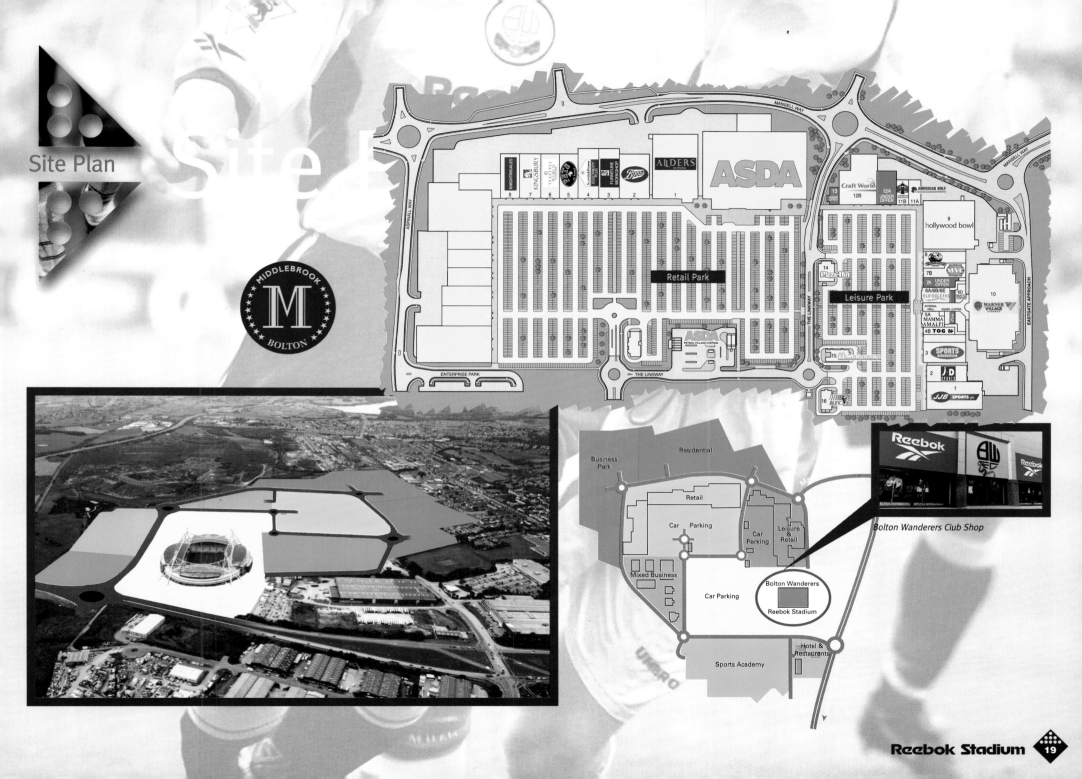

Site Plan

MIDDLEBROOK
M
BOLTON

Bolton Wanderers Club Shop

The Emerson Group is over the oon at Bolton

WE have been prolific goal scorers for Bolton over the years.

'Kick-off' was in 1988 with our first residential development in Bolton rising steadily to a score of eight by 1998.

Out playing the competition on and off the park

THE EMERSON GROUP

(Sunninghill Park and Belmont Park to name but two!) has been the hallmark of our game.

Like Bolton, recent promotion has seen us move into a different league with our involvement in the Reebok Stadium and the Middlebrook leisure, retail and business parks.

As a result, you could say we're over the moon!

FOR MORE INFORMATION PLEASE CONTACT **Orbit** Developments FOR MIDDLEBROOK ON 01204 673100

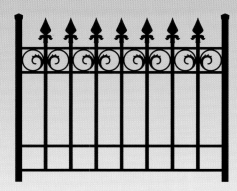

Paul Fletcher, Chief Executive Reebok Stadium

The End of an Era

BURNDEN PARK
1895 · 1997
THE END OF AN ERA

When a new Stadium opens, what can often be forgotten is the closure of the old Stadium. It is important to allows fans, especially fans who have spent most of their lives supporting the Club at one Stadium, to take part in the closure. And for them also to retain a treasured momento to remind them of great victories and happy times........ and also a few sad ones.

To commemorate the closure of Burnden Park the Directors of Bolton Wanderers Football Club commissioned thirteen initiatives which allowed not only fans of the Club, but also collectors and football enthusiasts nationwide to take part in the historic closure.

The events were organised under the banner 'Farewell to Burnden Park, the End of an Era', 1895-1997. Early planning began in late 1996 some six months prior to the Stadium's official closure on Friday 25th April 1997. Over 10,000 colour brochures including mail order forms were sent out to season ticket holders in February 1997 and by mid April over 10,000 orders had been received. The 13 initiatives were advertised as opposite.

The end of an era proved extremely successful. Amongst the highlights were ● Gold Programmes sold out within 3 days ● 160 fans bought a framed piece of the Board Room carpet ● over 100 teams with players of all ages from 8 to 80 played on Burnden Park ● Roll call fully subscribed ● Limited edition plates, 1000 sold in 4 weeks ● Over 140 fans bought a piece of Burnden Park Turf ● Over 2000 people attended the Grand Auction ● End of an Era Video included some archive footage from the early 1900's, never seen before by Wanderers fans.

10,000 Brochures sent out.

A commemorative programme was produced.

Play on Burnden Park.

Items from the Auction.

1. Book. Burnden Park - The Final Years 1987 - 1997

Burnden Park has seen many ups and downs for the Club none more so than in the last ten years. Burnden Park - The Final Years 1987-1997, covers that period with a full statistical analysis and pen pics of every player to have represented the Club in that period.

2. Grand Draw

Win one of the shirts worn by the players involved in the final game played at Burnden Park; there will be a total of 13 shirts to be won (5 draw tickets are enclosed).

3. Farewell Video

A 90 minute video appropriately entitled 'The Final Whistle' re-lives many special recorded moments at Burnden Park. The Final Whistle features exclusive footage from the BBC. Granada and archive film companies and has been produced on the highest standard broadcasting equipment. A collector's item and great present for any Wanderers fan.

4. Last Match Programme

A special A4 size, 68 page souvenir issue will be produced to mark the event. Commemorating 102 years of football at Burnden Park, this will be a must for fans and collectors alike. A limited edition of 1000 copies finished in gold are available for collectors.

5. Listing in the Final Match Programme

Secure your place in history - for just £5 your name will appear in the special 'I was There' roll call that will feature in the souvenir issue final match programme.

6. Play on Burnden Park

A once in-a-lifetime opportunity to tread the same turf as today's and yesterday's greats. For a limited period only, your team can play a 70 minute match at Burnden Park with full use of the Club's facilities, kit, referee, referee's assistants (linesmen!) and, if required, your opposition can also be provided.

7. Sportsmans Banquet and Sportsmans Dinner

In May 1997 the final Sportsmans Dinners will be staged in the Executive Club at Burnden Park. The Sportsmans 'Banquet' will be attended by great players from the past., while players from today's squad will be at the Sportsman's Dinner. Nat Lofthouse has donated items to auction at the Banquet.

8. Framed Limited Edition Prints

Internationally renowned sports artist Brian Halton has been commissioned to depict the final match on canvas and a limited number of high quality prints will be produced. Each print will be individually numbered and carry the signature not only of the aritist but also of Bolton's team that day and a number of Wanderers stars of the past.

9. Memorabilia Auction

With 102 years of history going under the hammer, this is your opportunity to be the proud owner of one of hundreds of highly collectable authentic Club items of memorabilia and ephemera.

10. Commemorative Merchandise

Our Club Shop has produced a selection of commemorative items designed to keep alive the memory of Burnden Park forever. From ties, mugs and clothing to posters and key rings, there is something for every taste, age and pocket, some items will be made from genuine material from Burnden Park.

11. Burnden Park Turf

Recreate the spirit of Burnden Park in your own garden by buying half a metre of the historic turf.

12. Boardroom Carpet

The Boardroom has been the location of countless historic events over the years and its carpet has been trodden by legends of football folklore. A number of sections carrying the unique BWFC logo will be framed and made available to supporters (two sizes available).

12a. Bone China Plate

A limited edition of 1000 Bone China Plates has been commissioned to depict the final league match at Burnden Park. Not only a lasting memory but a superb investment too.

October

Steelwork

The East Stand steelwork, the final shape can clearly be seen.

With the end of Autumn looming and less than twelve months to completion, the maintenance of the projects progression was paramount. Every hour and day of non-productivity would mean that this time was still to be made up. On a construction project, the thing that cannot be controlled is the weather and on a daily basis members of staff would apprehensively await the weather forecast for the forthcoming days.

Luckily, just as the summer and holiday suntans were wearing thin the sun decided to make a most welcome return to Middlebrook. With it a welcome boost to site progress and a source of inspiration for the much maligned site workforce, who by this time must have been wondering if the rain would manage to stop before the frost set in for the Winter.

The tonnes of steelwork that had landed on site were continuing to be assembled like a huge meccano set and with it the welcome sight of a frame that resembled a football stand.

Piling had continued throughout the period and with it the completion of the gigantic piles on which the floodlights would be sited.

The intricacies of the stadium design cannot be explained in a script such as this nor by anything penned by myself. However for those who managed to witness the construction of the mast bases in any way at all will concur with the magnitude that is beyond belief and a feat of structural engineering. The volume of concrete and steel required to construct the bases ensured countless late nights and lost weekends.

Steelwork and concrete are prepared for early start.

Luckily, just as the summer and holiday suntans were wearing thin the sun decided to make a most welcome return to Middlebrook

Piling takes place on the East Stand.

The East Stand starts to take shape as groundworks continue for the South Stand

Structural steelwork begins.

The relentless rainfall
had returned and our
October oasis had gone,

*Tons of steel to reinforce the floodlight
mast foundations.*

The Reebok Story

David Singleton -
Vice President Reebok UK

1995 saw the centenary of Reebok. Although not until years later was the name of Reebok adopted, the man who created the birth of a great Company was as innovative as his present day successors in the design of a product that was to influence the direction of sport.

In 1895 Joe Foster, a craftsman shoemaker from Bolton, was a keen runner and member of Bolton Primrose Harriers. In the search for a sporting lead he made, as legend would have it in his garden shed, the first simple pair of spiked running shoes that were little more than a pair of ordinary running shoes with nails crafted through the soles.

This gave him the winning edge when running on cinders and soft grass.

Nine years later, in 1904, a runner called Alf Shrub broke three World running records at different distances in one ten mile race wearing a pair of Joe Foster's running shoes. His record time was 50 minutes 40.6 seconds and his running shoes cost him the princely sum of five shillings and sixpence - twenty seven and a half pence in todays money.

Other World and Olympic medals followed rapidly for many different athletes.

The development of Foster's shoes took a back seat in 1914 with the outbreak of the First World War. The small factory turned to production of army boots to aid the war effort.

As soon as peace was restored to the World, Joe Foster renewed his interest in developing racing shoes and soon he was able to boast that many athletes were again winning Olympic medals wearing Foster's shoes. But perhaps the most famous was the Gold won by an

athlete - Lord Burghley - in 1928 wearing a pair of his spikes. Decades later, the feats of Lord Burghley and other athletes wearing Foster's shoes were to form the basis for the Oscar winning film 'Chariots of Fire.' Further sporting successes were to follow and by the time Joe died in 1933 Bolton Wanderers, Liverpool and Arsenal players were wearing Foster football boots.

Joe's great legacy was left to his sons John and James.

Recognising the opportunity provided by their father, the Foster boys expanded the range of sporting shoes into other areas, building the reputation of Foster's shoes for boxing, rugby, field events and road walking, with the small factory in Deane Road, Bolton, expanded and renamed 'The Olympic Works.'

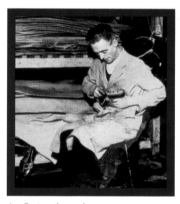

Joe Foster, shoemaker.

But 1939 halted the progress of the Company with a return to manufacturing army boots for the Second World War which, in 1943, saw the factory bombed and production stopped.

A new era began for the Foster family in 1948, when the new 'Olympic Works' was opened on a different site in Bolton and Joe Foster's two grandsons were apprenticed to the firm. As the decade of the 50's dawned, a hint of the international potential of Foster's sports shoes was evident when Moscow Dynamo - the first Soviet football team to visit the West - all wore Foster's boots.

But perhaps the greatest satisfaction for the family came in 1958, when Nat Lofthouse scored the winning goal against Manchester United in the FA Cup Final at Wembley wearing, of course, a pair of Foster's football boots.

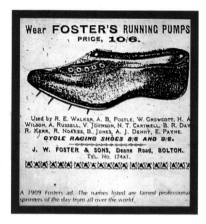

Early marketing of Foster's running shoes.

Reflecting on this period in the development of the Foster Sports Shoe business, Joe Foster Junior said, "We needed a brand name. I wanted an animal name and just had a feeling about the letter 'R.' So I went to the dictionary and found 'Reebok'...a fast and agile gazelle." In this simple way one of the World's greatest sports names was born.

Throughout the next two decades Reebok grew steadily, their running shoes remaining popular with top athletes. And with the boom in sport and fitness Reebok soon became known and worn in every country in the World.

Although synonymous with global sporting achievement, Reebok have always maintained the closest of links with both Joe Foster's home town and their famous football team, 'The Trotters.' As a player for both the Wanderers and England, Nat Lofthouse had worn Reebok boots, not because of sentimentality but because they were the best.

The partnership with Bolton Wanderer's began to flourish in 1987 when, in an FA Cup match against Forest, the Reebok logo first appeared on those famous white shirts as kit sponsors. Then, in 1990, Reebok confirmed its commitment by becoming Club sponsors.

As innovative as Joe Foster may have been, working alone in his garden shed just over a hundred years ago, he could not have dreamt that his work would ultimately lead to the creation of a name famous in sport throughout the World. Or that one day a magnificent Stadium would be built in his home town within walking distance from where the story began.

Just as Joe Foster created a sporting symbol at the end of the last century, The Reebok is a symbol for sport in the next century,

Graphic Design - Mike Trevena
Atom Design Associates

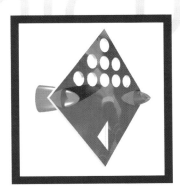

Left to right: Internal signage system visuals, utilising the Stadium logo. Stadium/BWFC branded wine bottles. Visuals showing how external signage could be applied using the floodlight mast and diamond shapes.

1996 saw the start of many changes for BWFC, the most significant of which was, of course, the move to a new home. From the initial plans, it was obvious that the visual impact of the stadium on the landscape and the local community was going to be immense. Never in its 102 illustrious years had the Club had the opportunity to make such a bold statement of its ambitions. It was at this stage that designs were submitted by Atom Design Associates with the intention of carrying this statement into the next millennium.

Today's emblem, designed by Mike Trevena of Atom, was chosen as a reflection of excitement and celebration, and was directly inspired by the visual images of supporters celebrating, with scarves and flags, Bolton's trip to Wembley for the Coca Cola cup final and the ongoing atmosphere on the team's return to Burnden Park. The ribbons, which bring movement, colour and excitement to the new emblem, are distinctive, unique and instantly recognisable, and are seen as being an integral part of any future marketing and club promotion.

Designers Atom have also taken full advantage of one of the Stadium's most distinctive architectural features: its floodlights. The now familiar diamond shape has provided an extremely strong visual image and it has been used to identify the Reebok stadium and its various 'products'. The diamond shape and ribbons lends itself to a host of applications ranging from internal signage systems such as those in the Middlebrook exhibition centre and function suites, to embossing on bars and a custom-designed pattern on carpeting.

Throughout the 'launch' and ongoing promotion of the Reebok Stadium and its ancillary facilities, all promotional material and graphics have made strong use of the new identity.

The ultimate goal.

Ian Anthony

Ian Anthony (Bolton) Ltd. 141/149 Bradshawgate, Bolton BL2 1BP Tel: 01204 399 633

Press Facilities - Alan Fullelove - Press & PR Officer

Match action pictures are wired direct from The Reebok into the newspaper office.

Photographers set up their equipment pre-match.

I n my capacity as Press Officer for Bolton Wanderers Football Club, I was given the task of designing and overseeing the installation of journalistic and photographic press facilities at the Reebok Stadium.

With almost 20 years experience of working in press boxes as a feature writer on various sports magazines and as a radio sports reporter, I was able to base my recommendations on practical first hand knowledge.

As far as I was concerned there were two major considerations to be borne in mind. Firstly that the football club should provide a clean, functional and comfortable working environment for the media. Secondly that seating within the press box area itself should allow ease of access and egress without unnecessary disturbance to fellow journalists.

Both these points were readily taken on board by the Wanderers' directors and the result is that working conditions for the media visiting The Reebok Stadium are recognised as being among the finest in the country.

International, national, regional and local journalists representing newspapers, magazines, radio and TV are based on the third floor of the main West stand. This area is accessed by lift or stairs from the main reception area and the media has use of two spacious rooms before the game, at half-time and post-match. Adequate refreshments are available to visiting pressmen from an hour before kick-off and this is certainly welcomed by those who may have travelled for several hours by road or rail to the game.

Press stewards are on hand to direct journalists to one or other of the 70 seats in the working area of the press box. The stewards also supply programmes and team changes along with any other relevant information that may be required.

Each seat at the desk space in the working area of the Reebok Stadium press box is fitted with both electrical power points and a telephone line. Several national newspapers have installed their own telephone points in the box while radio and television positions have been provided with modern ISDN, broadcast quality equipment. Very little, if anything, has been ignored from the original plan submitted to the board.

That is very definitely the case when one considers facilities at the Reebok for press photographers.

Based in the Stadium's North-East tunnel, some 40 press photographers can be accommodated in the photographer's wire-room. From this base pictures can be wired to newspaper offices all over the world using one or other of the 21 wire points provided by the club.

Press articles, reports and pictures play a major role in developing and maintaining interest in the game of professional football. No other sport can command as many column inches or hours of airtime. That is particularly true with the blanket coverage now given by Sky Television and TV facilities received a great deal of consideration as the Reebok Stadium was being developed.

BBC, Sky and Granada were all involved in several meetings to decide and approve parking areas for outside broadcast vehicles, routes for running camera and sound cables, size and accessibility of overhead camera gantry, position of permanent TV studio and post-match interview area and the number and exact positions of camera points around the playing area.

The outcome of the hours of time and effort is, we believe, a Stadium that is media friendly and one that provides a clean, comfortable working environment for all press representatives be they in newspapers, radio or television.

Local, national and international journalists have a stunning view of the action.

Photography by David Taylor
Panoramic Photographer to leading Football clubs throughout Europe.
For further information contact: DAVID TAYLOR: 0374 949997
SPECTRUM COLOUR SOLUTIONS LIMITED: 01249 444404

Reebok Stadium 57

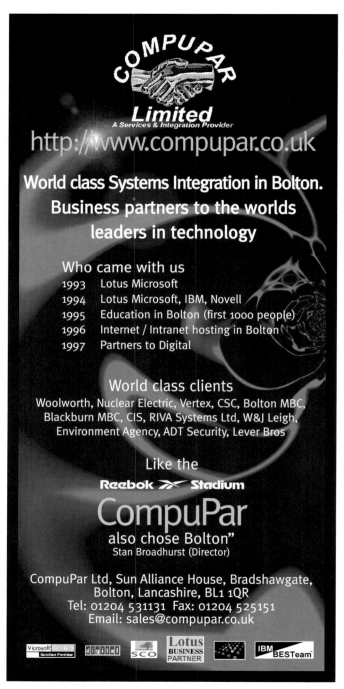

January **97**

Concrete Terracing

The turning of the year saw the project reach a stage of construction which signified that even after six months of hard work, the site team had made commendable progress. The next eight months of the project would always be the most crucial of the project, but in more ways than one the foundations for completion had already been laid.

There was still a considerable amount of design work to be completed and with it the final interiors scheme for the by now fully subscribed executive areas. The period was to draw on the resources and character of all the site team and the completion would require a display of effort and resilience from all involved.

Over the next eight months the project would test many of the strong willed and would effect the lives of all those committed to the scheme. The Stadium would be responsible for many a late night and weekend, and with it would put a strain on the home lives of the team. Of course the effort would be rewarded by the ultimate completion but the time lost with families would be lost forever.

The project entered a phase of focusing on the buildings external appearance; cladding, brickwork/blockwork and roofing. In the same stage the roof steelwork became fully positioned and the huge steel masts that would site the stadiums floodlighting would be positioned.

Contracting can be frought with problems and to say the project was devoid of any would not give the credit to the site staff who dealt with each and everyone. The magnitude of the co-ordination of tasks and the requirement to ensure activities were completed by due dates required a high level of management skills. Sometimes management is not always about how well you can plan and organise, but it is also how best to deal with one off instances as and when they arrive.

Site motivation was kept to as high a level as possible with continued visits to the local taverns and regular five a side tournaments. Our performances varied in quality terms but on occasion Colin Todd may have had the opportunity to view some new talent. Apparently, Colin could not manage to observe our Monday night efforts as he was then preoccupied with the talents of a former England World Cup star playing in the North East of England.

The steelwork starts to span the corners.

Props hold up the roof

Over the next eight months the project would test many of the strong willed and would affect the lives of all those committed to the scheme

The first piece of the exposed roof steel work arrives on site.

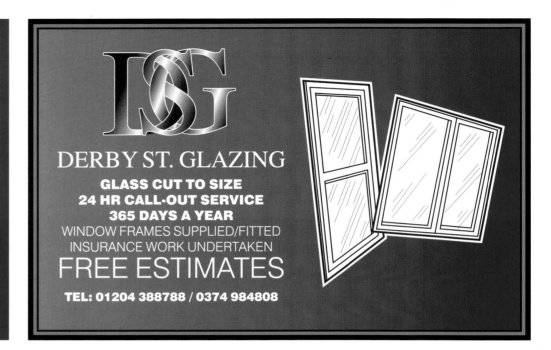

Dressing Rooms - Andrew Hobson
Design Consultant

L ike many other aspects of the Stadium, the dressing rooms, players and officials facilities are of a standard never seen before in British stadia. The latest FIFA and UEFA guidelines require four specific requirements all of which are included within the Reebok Stadium design.

1. Dressing Rooms

Both the home and away dressing rooms need to be identical. Gone are the days when the home changing room was immaculate with marble walls and the visitors were offered little more than a storeroom.
Gone also is the large 'plunge' bath evident at old stadiums.
At the Reebok players have the option of showers or individual slipper baths. Although the dressing rooms are of a basic design they are both spacious and comfortable.

2. Warm Up Room

The latest guidelines also require a 'kick about area' or warm up room, within the dressing room area. Again these facilities are included at the Reebok measuring 50 sq. metres. The home team dressing room links into the warm up area which directly leads to the physiotherapy room and doctors office.
These areas are also linked into the assistant managers office, trainers office and managers office. The manager also has private showers and changing facilities.

3. Separate 'Run Out Tunnels'

The Stadium design also features separate 'run out tunnels' for both the home and visiting teams. The origin of this requirement is thought to be the need to illiminate any confrontation between the players as they leave the field of play.

4. Female Officials Room

How long will it be before we see the first female referee take control of a Premier League game?
Probably not as long as we think. Any new Stadium built for the next century needs to provide separate changing facilities for female officials and again these facilities are included at the Reebok.

Other points to note:

- Around the playing surface you will find a red 'tartan' track, similar to the surfaces used for athletics. This not only provides a superb training area for players but the surface also helps keep the seats clean as it is dust free.
- The Reebok Stadium also has a drugs testing room and T.V. Interview Room alongside the players changing facilities. Press interview room and press facilities are on level three.

The players dressing room.

The Reebok Stadium's physiotherapy facilities are some of the best in the country

The red 'tartan' track, similar to the surfaces used for athletics.

Reebok Ticket Office

Graham Holliday
Ticket Office Manager

Ticketing plays an extremely important part in the administration of modern day football. Not only does a ticket admit you into the Stadium it also ensures that you have a reserved seat.

With the Reebok Stadium being all-seater, every seat has to be registered on the clubs computer system. This is to ensure that every seat can be accounted for; and when games are sold out the club cannot sell tickets and exceed the capacity. A similar control was applicable at Burnden Park for several seasons, where local safety authorities strictly monitored standing capacity.

After the tragic accident at Hillsborough, the call for stern safety procedures was heard. Before the disaster, ground regulations were somewhat basic. All-ticket matches were very infrequent and terraces were always crammed at very popular matches. The vast majority of fans paid at the turnstiles to stand up, leaving only a few using tickets to sit down in allocated seats. The attendance was totalled by calculating the clock-counter system on the turnstiles and by adding up the ticket stubs from ticket-only stiles. Using this method it was impossible to regulate how many people were being admitted at any given time leading up to kick-off.

With the advancement of modern technology, not only was it possible to scrutinise the number of spectators being admitted, but also to print the tickets in-house. Prior to the season beginning 1992/93, everything was done by hand. Season ticket holders were logged in to a book and tickets were bulk-printed on a basic P.C. When fans requested certain seats, ticket office staff had to search through lots of pre-printed tickets to find the designated seat. Payment on the turnstiles accounted for the majority of attendance. The number of season ticket holders was at most a couple of thousand.

The success on the field coincided with the club investing in a computerised ticketing system. This saw the demise of the archaic P.C. and brought in an efficient mechanised process for selling tickets. People could now look on the monitor and select an available seat and within a couple of seconds the ticket was in their hands. This new method got rid of the need to print tickets in bulk. This proved valuable in terms of time and wastage.

Photograph: Ian Lawson

The number of season ticket holders grew as the football team climbed up the leagues. Fortunately, the new ticketing system catered for this. Every season ticket holder had an individual file whereby certain information was available to the operator. Such as their seat number and address. Renewing season tickets at the start of the new season was never as simple. Gone were the days when you had to re-write the data into a brand new book. All that was required now was a simple press of a button and the information was automatically transferred. You can imagine how this dramatically reduced the queuing time. The storage capacity for the new system was put to its strongest test in 1995/96 season when the Wanderers were promoted to the Premier League. A staggering 15,000 people invested their cash into purchasing season tickets - a two fold increase on the previous year.

The rise in the number of spectators who bought season tickets meant that tickets available to the general public were in short supply. For glamorous fixtures, lengthy queues were a common sight in and around Burnden Park. Most games in the Premier League became all-ticket.

With the closure of Burnden Park looming, the club decided to issue a special edition, commemorative ticket for the final game against Charlton Athletic. This ticket was designed by the ticket office and produced by an external company.

The move to the Reebok Stadium proved an administrative headache for all the staff at Burnden. Due to a very strict time scale, the ticket office staff had to sell season tickets, even before the seats were physically in place. This was problematic in the sense that the fans could not view their seat before they bought them. The ticket office staff had to individually create a ticket map onto the main computer system by using architects plans.

After the first ever game at the brand new stadium, it became apparent that some season ticket holders had bought seats that did not actually exist. This brought anxiety to both parties. Eventually, when the dust settled, fans were relocated.

With technology spiralling the future looks extremely promising for the football fan. At some stage it should be possible to buy a ticket in the same way you withdraw money from a cash-till. It is just around the corner.

BOLTON WANDERERS.1 NEWCASTLE.0
1/12/1997. Attendance: 25,000

Photography by David Taylor
Panoramic Photographer to leading Football clubs throughout Europe.
For further information contact: DAVID TAYLOR: 0374 949997
SPECTRUM COLOUR SOLUTIONS LIMITED: 01249 444404

Stadium Design - LOBB Sports Architecture

Rod Sheard
Chairman, Lobb Sports Architecture

Sydney, Australia.

Sydney, Australia.

On the 1st September 1997 the Reebok Stadium hosted its first football match. The Stadium, a new home for Bolton Wanderers Football Club, opened its doors to a capacity 25,000 all ticket crowd and, via Sky TV, a far larger remote audience around the world. This is the essence, the function of the modern Stadium, leisure and entertainment centres to the live audience who have taken the trouble to attend and a television studio to that remote electronic audience who may be enjoying the same event from anywhere on earth where television is broadcast. The Reebok Stadium is a global building and its influence extends far beyond the M61 from which it appears in the distance as some futuristic disc inviting spectators to enter.

The Bolton v Everton match was not great sport but the event itself can never be relied upon to entertain, that is why the new breed of stadia the Reebok Stadium represents is focused on providing a level of entertainment value far beyond its predecessors. The building is about providing a comfortable, entertaining and safe environment for thousands of people for several hours at a time.

The following day after the opening match the national press was full of compliments for the Club's ambition on its return to the top of English football, the Premier League and particularly for the vision embodied in the design of its new Stadium. Bolton Wanderers had been looking to move from their 102 year old home at Burnden Park for a number of years. Burnden Park was Bolton's second home after Pike's Lane from where they were one of the twelve founding members of the first football league in 1888. Burnden Park had a colourful history, suffering one of football's saddest occasions when on 9th March 1946, a total of 33 people died at the Railway End due to crushing.

Brief

The clients aspirations were for a football Stadium which primarily could offer superior viewing, comfort and safety standards to all spectators and one which could also make an architectural statement to help give the club the profile and identity it desired. It also needed to be multi-functional, using its many planned facilities for other than football use. The Stadium had to accommodate restaurants, shops, conference facilities, exhibition spaces, a nursery and medical facilities. The Local Authority were supportive of the concept of a new Stadium and desired an indoor community sports facility to form part of the venue, preferably built into the actual stands. This hall needed to be large enough to be used for exhibitions and shows but also indoor sports such as netball and basketball.

Site

LOBB Sports Architecture were first involved in the project in 1994 after the club had been considering a new venue for some time and had entered into discussions with the local council in order to identify an appropriate site. A site near Horwich on the outskirts of Bolton was identified which benefited from close proximity to junction 6 of the M61 motorway, giving it good road links to Manchester, Liverpool and Leeds via the M62, Preston and the North from the M6. Plans were also put in place for a new railway station to be added to the railway line which runs close to the site.

A key factor in the council support of the development was the promise of up to 3,000 new permanent jobs the development would bring to the area in addition to the tangible financial benefits of a huge construction project and the temporary employment that brought.

The design has taken its place in a comprehensive development, known as Middlebrook, being an overall 200 acre site, occupying the most prominent, road frontage location as the flagship building. It is also physically linked to the adjoining leisure building offering an extensive network of leisure related facilities.

Melbourne, Australia.

Design Concept

The design of the Stadium represents an incremental advance on LOBB's award winning Stadium in Huddersfield. The client had visited this venue and recognised the exciting style of venue they were looking for with the one significant variation of designing the lower tier as a complete and continuous bowl. All seats are under cover and within 90 metres of the centre of the field. They all have 'C' values of 90 mm or more, providing a wonderful clear view of the whole pitch, from every seat. Thanks to the extensive site available the Stadium could have its own, ground level, 25 metre wide pedestrian concourse (the Piazza) surrounding the venue which fulfils several functions. It provides a circulation route between the various entrances; can accommodate external concessions and pre-match entertainment and provides a clearly defined 'place of safety' in case of emergency.

To respond to the clients ambitions of achieving a 'landmark' structure LOBB's developed a form of building which visually focused on a dramatic roof over-sailing a simple but articulate oval bowl. The bowl itself would be continuous in a large oval plan form providing constantly changing perspectives from any point of view. The roof itself was conceived as a series of four leaning tapering tube towers providing support for the pitch floodlighting, and the main roof trusses which spanned to full length of each side. The trusses themselves are curved both top and bottom to reflect the true viewing nature of the bowl below and the natural structural integrity of the structural element. The composition achieves a floating scalloped canopy over the bowl each element fitting neatly to the other and being read as one unified form.

The West stand contains on ground level public areas including the main concourse with its many associated facilities. It is also a service and administration floor containing offices for the club and the stadium management and changing and warm-up facilities for players. Level 1 includes the Chairman's Suite, Boardroom and Directors Guest Lounge. The Wanderers Suite (Players Bar) and office accommodation. A main production kitchen is also situated to the South. Level 2 above accommodates a second concourse, served by dedicated twin sets of scissors stairs and the Stadium's private boxes, and a banqueting suite capable of providing seated dining for 450 people. Level 3 is another public concourse providing access to the upper tier of viewing and level 4 is plant area containing engineering services.

The East stand houses most of the Stadium's community facilities with ground and first floors accommodating the large double height sport and exhibition space. Level 2 is devoted to club and private box holders facilities; the Lion of Vienna Suite; Hall of Fame Suite and Burnden Lounge, which is planned to open in early 1998.

The North stand is the 'home' end of Bolton Wanderers' supporters and backs onto a 3,000 space car park. Ground floor accommodates the public concourse, and it is intended later to house club, retail and and club restraurant while Level 1 is planned for food and beverage areas. Level 2 accommodates a concourse and accommodation overlooking the playing surface that could be let as office space.

The South stand is the 'visitors' end of the ground backing onto its own car park. Internal circulation is similar to that of the North stand and the building can be subdivided into sections to allow for varying numbers of visiting fans. Escape time for all the stands in case of emergency is calculated at below 8 minutes from any seat to a 'place of safety' which is the wide public concourse.

Atmosphere

Emphasis was placed on the Stadium possessing a good 'football atmosphere'. The general perception is that it is up to the players on the pitch to produce exciting football in order to lift the crowd and so create 'atmosphere', but LOBB's specialist knowledge of this building type allows this to assist this process by carefully designing Stadia which generate their own atmosphere. Judging by the crowds reaction since its opening these ideas are clearly working.

It is intended, like most new stadia, that the Reebok will be much more than a football ground used once a fortnight, but will be a leisure complex, centring on the football team, and operate seven days per week. There are extensive facilities 'below' such as the 46 executive boxes, a Banqueting Suite which can seat 450 people, lounges of various sizes around the ground. An unusual feature which is not evident externally is the huge 35,000 square feet of double height exhibition space under the East stand, which has a clear 8 metre ceiling height. General spectator access is gained through turnstiles set in the perimeter wall. In each corner of each stand are two banks of turnstiles and exit gates; one set exclusively serving the lower tier and the other serving the upper tier.

Separate VIP access is available to both the West and East stands' executive areas at level 2. It is intended that the different executive areas can be utilised on a daily basis. In future the Club can consider alternative uses such as office accommodation. themed restaurants; medical and sports injury rehabilitation units to the levels of the North and South stands.

This Reebok Stadium has probably the best circulation of any football stadium in the country. Not only is there excellent vertical circulation but the whole Stadium has uninterrupted service circulation on the lowest three levels but with access available all around at upper concourse level also. For the Stadium operators this makes management so much easier, as they can access all levels at all times without leaving the building. Another unique feature that has probably never been seen before in any Stadium is the twin player tunnels. The intention is for the two teams to be able to enter the field and be introduced individually, so highlighting the sense of theatre and so atmosphere.

Conclusion

The Reebok Stadium is unquestionably a landmark building that has been quickly adopted by Bolton's supporters as their 'spiritual home'. Many have suggested that the Reebok would never have been designed as it is was not for the precedent Huddersfield set in the development of their new Stadium, a Stadium which went on to win the coveted award of RIBA Building of the Year in 1995. But to see this new venue in the shadow of Huddersfield would be wrong. The Reebok is strikingly different, bigger and more integrated in its concept providing the extensive facilities required for the modern Premier League Club, it is an assertive, individual statement which stands alone in the history of Stadium development.

There are about five years between LOBB's design for this Stadium and their well known work at Huddersfield and it is interesting to compare the development thought and application between the two buildings. Huddersfield was designed for clubs with fewer financial resources capable of being brought to bear on the project. The Reebok Stadium is therefore a more extensive development and designed to be built in one main phase of work with smaller stages of infill which would not require major structural additions while Huddersfield was designed to be built in four distinct phases because of the limited funds available at its initial inception.

Huddersfield broke the ground for expressive football stadia in the UK, stadia which communicate to their arriving spectators while they are still in their car some distance from the grounds saying 'this is a place of excitement and entertainment, you are going to enjoy yourself here'. The Reebok Stadium is certainly a proud landmark which 'speaks' to its arriving fans with a clear message, a message of progress and success, a message the Bolton Wanderers Football Club clearly envisaged in 1994 when they took the first brave steps to move from their long established home. The extensive flexibility designed into the Stadium reaches their maximum potential together, a future which looks very promising.

Currently Lobb Sports Architecture are working on the new Sydney Stadium in Australia in readiness for the 2,000 olympic games. The illustration on this page shows the next generation at new stadium borne out of The Reebok.

Transport Strategy

John Walsh O.B.E.
Transport Consultant

The move to a new Stadium after more than 100 years of football at Burnden Park was bound to change the habits of a lifetime and Bolton Wanderers recognised that the move to a new Stadium would require a combination of transport arrangements.

As far back as 1995, the Club undertook its first survey of travel needs. A detailed study of the postal addresses of season ticket holders and members, enabled a detailed profile of the geographic spread of regular spectators at Burnden Park to be established. Apart from a small number of fans who were registered at addresses as far apart as Inverness and Plymouth, the vast majority lived within the greater Bolton area. From this profile, it was possible to plan bus routes to cover not just Bolton itself, but also surrounding areas.

A network of 14 routes ensured that the vast majority of fans had a reasonably local bus service to enable them easily to get to the new Stadium. Discussions with local bus operators took place when the routes were agreed and a flat rate fare of £1 was felt to be the best option to ensure speedy loading.

Although several thousands now travel by bus, the car was always going to be the principal mode of transport. Discussions were held with Police and Local Authority about the car parking strategy and so began another exercise, selling hundreds of tickets for car parks which were still at that time under construction.

Despite the large number of car parking spaces available, Bolton Wanderers recognised that even more would be needed. An offer was made by British Aerospace to open and operate around 1,000 additional spaces, with the proceeds going to charity.

The offer from a local school to provide additional car parking caused some concern to residents, and it was ultimately agreed to restrict the facility to Staff only parking. This was yet another important piece in a complex jigsaw.

The new roadworks around the site, such as. Chorley New Road and De Haviland Way, all have cycle lanes. This provides yet another means for fans to travel to matches.

Throughout, the needs of pedestrians have not been overlooked. Footpath links from Chorley New Road to the Stadium were planned; these were not available until more recently but, nonetheless, pedestrian traffic from Horwich has now been satisfied.

Many fans walk from Blackrod and Westhoughton. Again their needs have been accommodated with new footpaths and pedestrian safety rails along De Haviland Way towards the M61 motorway.

In less than six months, Bolton Wanderers now operates the largest number of car parking spaces of any Premier League Club in the country, and provides a unique system of bus services covering the whole of the area. A far cry indeed from the old days!

A p r i l 97
C l a d d i n g

Pre-formed concrete blocking starts to give the now familiar terracing.

The stadium now moved at a frenzied pace with the construction process preparing to reach its dramatic climax.

Cladding, roofing, blockwork. brickwork, mechanical and electrical installations continued on site and with them the continuing change in the stadium's appearance. It was definitely no longer a building site, it had evolved into a project that was living up to the expectations and high standards set for it. The project now looked like the stadium that so many of its avid followers had discussed during the previous months. Seats began to find their position within their designated stand and with it a lifetime of viewing for their respective user. As season tickets were purchased, prospective spectators were keen to find out the location of their seat. It was a little too early for this yet but I had already commenced my own mission impossible, to test drive every seat in the stadium, (It was a hard job, but somebody had to do it).

Before you begin to think that us on a site have nothing better to do all day, I never achieved my mission.

Left: The teams colours are clad onto East Stand.

However, having viewed the pitch from such obscure angles as the west stand roof and the floodlight masts, I settled for my favourite resting place, the front row of the upper level of the west stand-right on the half way line.

Meanwhile, back at the pitch level the former Prime Minister, Mr John Major had arrived on site. In the month ahead I am sure that this was one of Mr Major's better days, meeting Nat Lofthouse, Colin Todd, and being given the honour of walking on the hallowed turf. I am sure Mr Major enjoyed the opportunity to put into place the first floodlight diamond on top of the floodlight mast at the South East corner of the Stadium. His handling of the crane was quite superb!

The floodlights had arrived and glazing units were being installed with the cladding panels. The pitch remained in good condition in the early spring sun and with it a premier team stadium taking shape.

The roof starts to take its distinctive shape.

*Left: The exposed
steelwork to the roof
is near completion.*

Cladding, roofing,
blockwork, brickwork,
mechanical and
electrical installations
continued on site and
with them the
continuing change in
the stadium's
appearance

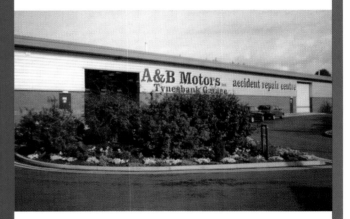

Better by Far -
By Paul Fletcher
Chief Executive
Reebok Stadium

Almost a decade has now passed since the football disasters of the late 1980's forced the Government to have an inquiry into the state of the Nations professional Stadia.

Looking back, the Taylor Report has been a great success. This study, linked to grant funding from the Football Trust has allowed Clubs to provide safe, comfortable Stadiums for their spectators, without risking their league position. This last point is quite an important one. Prior to the Taylor Report and the obligations that spectators had to be seated, most Clubs were more likely to spend money on players than on their Stadium's facilities.

The old Burnley Chairman, Bob Lord, thought he was a visionary who could break the mould. He rebuilt the old Turf Moor Stadium in the early 1970's. This put the Club in such financial difficulties that once the youth policy dried up around 1978 and players could not be sold to pay off the debts, the Club slid down to the bottom of the Fourth Division and almost out of the Football League.

Following the Taylor Report it is recorded that around 66 Clubs out of the 92 thought relocation (moving ground to a new site) was a better option than redevelopment (refurbishing the current ground). Ten years later, only eleven Clubs have pulled it off.

The early relocations of Scunthorpe, Walsall, Northampton and Chester were pretty straightforward affairs with normally the Club selling their old ground for enough money to build a similar sized Stadium. Then followed a group of more imaginative Stadia with Millwall, Huddersfield and Middlesbrough, each looking to build something more than just a Stadium for football.

The latest wave of Stadia involving Derby, Sunderland, Stoke and of course Bolton will become the best and possibly the last this century and bring the Taylor Report to a successful conclusion.

Since I visited the Toronto Sky Dome in 1990, I have been involved in new Stadia development, and in my opinion the Reebok Stadium is by far the best in this country . . . . in almost every aspect.

Probably it would have proved an easier and cheaper option to cram 40,000 seats into a traditional 'shoe box' design with four independent stands and not much else. But the visionaries on the Board at Bolton Wanderers had a much more businesslike approach and rather than re-inventing the wheel, visited dozens of new Stadiums and new stands to pick up inspirations and learn from early mistakes.

The Reebok Stadium therefore provides some of the finest spectator facilities to be found anywhere in Europe. So on the first visit on the 1st September 1997 Wanderers fans had a few items to look out for.

The Pitch
- You will not see much of the £400,000 investment, most of which is below the surface, but a mixture of 70% sand; 30% soil allows superb drainage. The long root, underground heating and sprinkler system could probably take three matches a week.

The Track
- Made from similar material to the new Tartan Running Tracks; this 'spring' surface not only provides a quality running track but is also dust free (this keeps the seats a lot cleaner in the lower tier).

Pitch Perimeter Signage
- A new system allows vertical advertising to the T.V. cameras (all these are taken by the Premier League for their core sponsors) measuring 2' x 20" with the reverse an angled board pointing to spectators (do not miss the important 'Don't go on the pitch' and 'Let's kick racism out of football' messages).

The Goal Posts
- I am sure the serious football spectators will not miss the new posts and nets. Without doubt the best nets for seeing the ball hit the net, ala Euro 96!

The Seats
- are a traditional moulded plastic but the 'steppings' (the distance between each row of seats) provide the most generous in British Football at 800 mm over 2' 6". If you do not believe me try sitting in the new stand at Elland Road!

The Concourses
- 8 spacious concourses, each allowing easy access between seats, toilets and food concessions.

For Disabled
- every area of the Stadium has been designed to cater for people with disabilities. The large areas pitchside in front of the Main Stand (home supporters end) and in front of the Bolton Evening News Stand provide easy access for Wanderers fans in wheelchairs. These slightly raised areas also offer a great view within 10 metres of play. Similar facilities are available for away supporters. For Wanderers wheelchair supporters an upper tier viewing position, behind glass is available in the North East Corner with a lift access, kindly sponsored by B.T. There is also a low level counter included at the ticket office. For supporters who have visual impairments a loop system links into the Stadium match broadcast at three front row locations for both home and away supporters, again sponsored by B.T.

Televisions
- Over 100 T.V. monitors are scattered around the Stadium showing both the build up to the game (from 1.15 pm onwards) up to kick off time when the match is shown live, so do not be scared to buy a coffee during the match, you will not miss any goals.

The Concessions (Kiosks)
- Operated by Gardner Merchant as part of their Stadium Catering Contract provide a good selection of food and refreshments. Fifteen of the concessions also offer beers and lagers - which of course must not be consumed in view of the pitch - and I know the John Smith's and McEwans brands will be very popular.

Statistics show that the most popular football spectators meal is a 'Pie and a Pint' and there will be adequate choice in the 'Mahoney's Kiosks' and 'Fast Eddies' pie bars.

Continued on page 105

Waste Bins - Are banned from most Football Stadiums but please use the plastic containers for all your waste paper and plastic glasses.

Electronic Scoreboard - or Video Screens as they are now called are located in the South East corner of the Stadium between the Nat Lofthouse Stand sponsored by Matthew Browns and the Visitors South Stand (yet to be named). Scoreboards have moved quickly from black and white bulb technology; to colour bulb/computer technology to the Jumbotron - as used at Highbury and White Hart Lane to . . . . . The Reebok Stadium, which features the very, very latest in L.E.D. technology imported from China via Milan to Bolton. If ever the Premier League will allow video screens to help the referee make decisions we are ready and waiting.

Executive Box and Hospitality Suite Holders - the 46 individual suites, again provide superb facilities which include the three key requirements for companies wanting to entertain guests at matchdays.

Research shows they have:-

1. Comfortable seats outside the suite to allow guests to get the full atmosphere of the game.

2. Good food and service within a spacious suite.

3. Private bars outside the suite to allow box holders to meet (and network) with other suite holders and their guests.

And on top of this, the Reebok Stadium suites offer a few added features which may not be noticeable, but all are very important.

- Outside the suite a 7' drop to spectator seating stops spectators turning around to look into the suite to see the action replay of the goal, shown on the T.V. inside the suite. This causes serious problems at other new stadia.

- The first tier of seats on the balcony outside the suites are one step below the suite itself. This allows guests to stay in the suite if they wish and get a clear view of the match without being obstructed by guests sitting in the seats outside the suite.

- Each suite has its own waiter/waitress for the day plus a hospitality host/hostess who looks after Suiteholders 'every need' via a call button.

- Each Suite has its own colour T.V. with Sky; Terrestrial and live football channel;

- Each Suite has a fridge and adequate hanging space for coats.

- The four private bars that support the suites are named:-
  The Presidents Bar - Main Stand - Presidents Suite.
  The Hopkinson Bar - Main Stand - Executive Suites.
  The Matthew Brown Bar - Nat Lofthouse Stand - Matthew Brown Suites.
  The Foweracre Bar - Nat Lofthouse Stand - Hall of Fame Suites.

It will not just be the last, it will be better by far than any of its predecessors . . . . by a mile.

Paul Fletcher, Chief Executive Reebok Stadium
One month prior to opening in September 1997.

For supporters who have joined the Clubs, again superb facilities will add to a great day out watching Premier League Football.

For Platinum Club Members - a magnificent Banqueting Suite in the main West Stand, centrally located in between the Presidents and Executive Suites, provides an air conditioned buffet lunch in one of the finest settings in the Premier League. Four large bars each within easy reach of the live action T.V. will become the place for after match celebrations or commiserations. For the match, the best cushioned seats in the house are reserved in the upper and lower tiers.

For Lion of Vienna Club Members - similar larger suite in the Nat Lofthouse Stand provides a great facility for fans who may not want to eat at every game. A buffet, or bar snack meal is available as are similar facilities to those in the Platinum Club with central seats for the match in the upper tier of the Nat Lofthouse Stand.

Match Sponsors - are located in a plush suite on level two between the Platinum Club and Presidents Suites. This room can accommodate a minimum of 20 up to a maximum of 50 sponsors guests. Its private bar adjoins the President Bar and is one of eleven independent bars within the Stadium.

The McDonalds Family Enclosure - recently sponsored by fast food giants McDonalds, features the only food concession in the Stadium which does not sell alcohol, this area of around 3,000 seats is serviced by two food concession points (one does sell alcohol) and is located in the upper tier of the Bolton Evening News Stand.

If there were another three pages available I could write about the hundreds of other similar advantages the Reebok Stadium has over other recent Stadiums.

Although Everton are starting to talk about leaving Goodison, I am sure it will not happen this century, if at all, which could leave the Reebok Stadium as the last of the Stadiums which have resulted from the Taylor Report. It will not just be the last, it will be **better by far** than any of its predecessors . . . . by a mile.

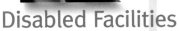

Disabled Facilities

BT

Liam O'Connor
Vice Chairman
BWFC Disabled
Supporters Association

Specially deigned access and seating facilities for disabled supporters.

E ven though Burnden Park was almost 100 years old and not designed for wheelchairs or disabled people, from my early days as a supporter, the club was always prepared to listen and provide the best possible facilities whenever possible. I am delighted that this process has continued at the new Reebok where myself and many other disabled fans are able to watch football amongst some of the finest facilities in Europe.

At Burnden I remember initially sitting behind the manager's dug out. It was a great place to watch football and listen to the manager's choice language. As more disabled fans started to attend matches we were then relocated into the Great Lever End. But always we entered the Stadium through the players tunnel and it was a particular thrill to get to know some players personally.

Initially, when I became disabled I was very depressed and football provided for me a great focus. Not only the football itself but I became involved in disabled issues regarding football. I am now delighted to be Vice-Chairman of the Bolton Wanderers Disabled

Supporters Association and represent Bolton Wanderers Football Club on the National Committee. Our organisation is officially recognised by the club, and the club always consult and listen when we have strong views on a subject.

It was obviously a great privilege, when we realised that Burnden Park would close, to be involved in helping to design facilities at the new Stadium. In the very early days we met with Director Graham Ball, Chief Executive Des McBain and PR Officer Alan Fullelove who went on to become the President of our Association.

We realised that we were representing not only the current Wanderers fans but also disabled supporters from future generations who would use the Stadium. We needed to get it right.

Alan Roberts BT, Nat Lofthouse President BWFC and Kevin Prince from the B.W.D.S.A. after the official unveilling.

Now that it is open we are delighted. To us it is the eighth wonder of the world. But, like other areas of the Stadium we have had our teething problems. Nevertheless, through meeting and talking them through we have been able to iron these out.

I suppose our problems are quite obvious. Parking, drop off points, easy access to the Stadium and toilets, good views and special needs for our blind and hard of hearing supporters. Superb access is available via a special corner door which leads directly to a slightly raised concrete platform to the North East corner of the ground. From car park to viewing position not one step!

It is possible to watch the match either from a side view about 5 metres from the touchline (40 wheelchair positions), or from a position behind the goals (32 wheelchair positions). Visiting fans have a similar facility behind the goals at the South of the Stadium with 32 wheelchair positions being available. Disabled helpers can sit directly behind on the front row of the Stadium unless they want to sit alongside when the club provide chairs on request.

We also benefit from a superb upper tier viewing facility kindly sponsored by British Telecom aptly named The B.T. Suite and officially opened by Club President Nat Lofthouse OBE . This glass fronted suite sits alongside the clubs executive boxes on level two in the North East corner. It accommodates 30 wheelchair users plus their helpers and access is available via excellent lifts and dedicated corridors free of stairs or obstacles. A similar suite is planned for the South East corner of the Stadium.

The suite also has an induction loop system for supporters with vision impairments and a similar system is available pitchside for both home and away supporters. Again this system was kindly sponsored by B.T. but designed by ourselves and Bolton Wanderers.

As I originate from Dublin I suppose I should have become a Manchester United supporter. But Bolton Wanderers are my team and always will be. I never regret supporting this warm, friendly club. Bolton Wanderers Football Club have made me proud by their commitment not only by providing the town with one of the best Stadiums in Europe, but they have listened and delivered facilities for their disabled supporters which I am sure cannot be bettered in English football.

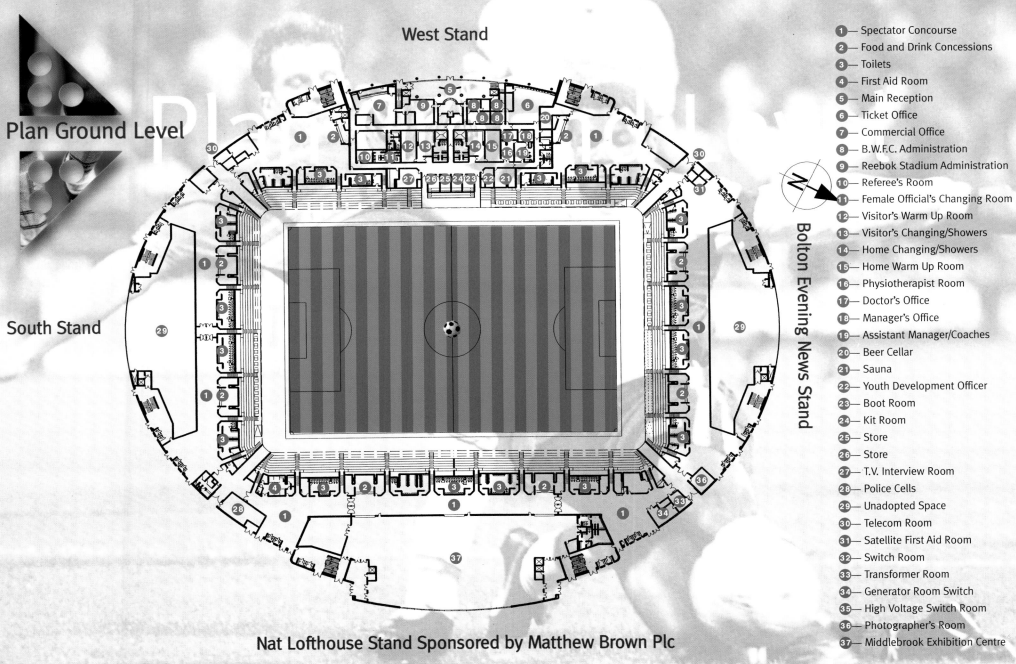

Plan Ground Level

West Stand

South Stand

Bolton Evening News Stand

Nat Lofthouse Stand Sponsored by Matthew Brown Plc

1 — Spectator Concourse
2 — Food and Drink Concessions
3 — Toilets
4 — First Aid Room
5 — Main Reception
6 — Ticket Office
7 — Commercial Office
8 — B.W.F.C. Administration
9 — Reebok Stadium Administration
10 — Referee's Room
11 — Female Official's Changing Room
12 — Visitor's Warm Up Room
13 — Visitor's Changing/Showers
14 — Home Changing/Showers
15 — Home Warm Up Room
16 — Physiotherapist Room
17 — Doctor's Office
18 — Manager's Office
19 — Assistant Manager/Coaches
20 — Beer Cellar
21 — Sauna
22 — Youth Development Officer
23 — Boot Room
24 — Kit Room
25 — Store
26 — Store
27 — T.V. Interview Room
28 — Police Cells
29 — Unadopted Space
30 — Telecom Room
31 — Satellite First Aid Room
32 — Switch Room
33 — Transformer Room
34 — Generator Room Switch
35 — High Voltage Switch Room
36 — Photographer's Room
37 — Middlebrook Exhibition Centre

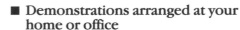

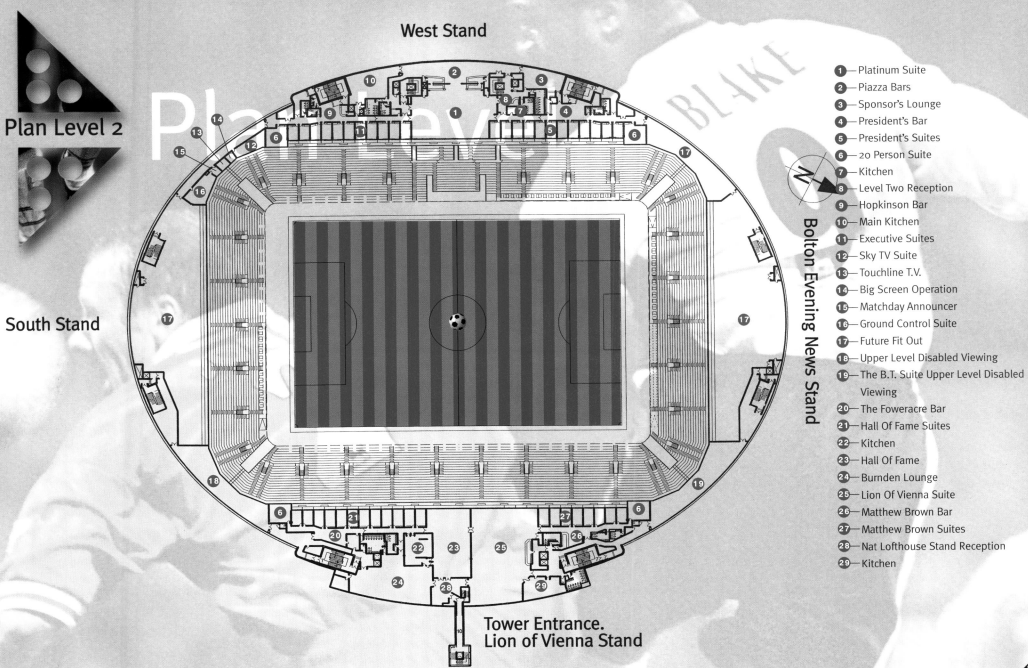

Plan Level 2

West Stand

South Stand

Bolton Evening News Stand

**Tower Entrance.
Lion of Vienna Stand**

1 — Platinum Suite
2 — Piazza Bars
3 — Sponsor's Lounge
4 — President's Bar
5 — President's Suites
6 — 20 Person Suite
7 — Kitchen
8 — Level Two Reception
9 — Hopkinson Bar
10 — Main Kitchen
11 — Executive Suites
12 — Sky TV Suite
13 — Touchline T.V.
14 — Big Screen Operation
15 — Matchday Announcer
16 — Ground Control Suite
17 — Future Fit Out
18 — Upper Level Disabled Viewing
19 — The B.T. Suite Upper Level Disabled Viewing
20 — The Foweracre Bar
21 — Hall Of Fame Suites
22 — Kitchen
23 — Hall Of Fame
24 — Burnden Lounge
25 — Lion Of Vienna Suite
26 — Matthew Brown Bar
27 — Matthew Brown Suites
28 — Nat Lofthouse Stand Reception
29 — Kitchen

May '97

External Work

Outside the stadium external work commences.

As the project entered into May, the four month countdown to completion began.

The stadium progress continued at a hectic pace with all areas of work being opened up to allow their respective activities to commence.

In the background to the site activity, the interior design scheme had been finalised and work was under way to ensure that the commitments given to ensuring quality would be achieved.

In and around the site other construction works were commencing with the need to ensure safe access to the stadium a priority. The Middlebrook development was beginning to look like a construction convention with a variety of contractors committed to ensure the completion of their respective parts.

The focal point and the centre piece of the development was and is undoubtedly The Reebok Stadium. The conglomeration of big name companies had only been enticed to the area by the fact that it would be home to one of Europe's premier stadiums.

The stadium itself was nearing ever closer to being watertight. Cladding panels and brickwork began to enclose the stands from the exterior whilst the inside had become enclosed by the positioning of the huge precast concrete terrace units which had now taken up their position in the stadium. The need to achieve a watertight building was essential to ensure that the finishes could commence in order to meet completion.

In the stands, a number of seats were taking their positions but it was still too early to appreciate the huge 'Reebok' design that would preoccupy the East stand seating. The pitch perimeter was being prepared in readiness for the perimeter running track that would see many a famous foot cross it. The structural steelwork operation neared completion but with it the presentation of another problem: How to paint the steelwork?

A gang of dedicated abseiling painters descended on site quite literally and would remain until every last beam had been given its coat of paint.

In each corner the floodlights were taking shape with huge scaffold towers being assembled to facilitate the assembly of the final installation.

Preparing for the arrival of the floodlight heads.

A gang of dedicated abseiling painters descended on site quite literally and would remain until every last beam had been given its coat of paint

The abseilers arrive on site.

External cladding takes the building one step nearer to completion.

An event to remember....

....A venue to match

- Full audio visual back up can be provided with precisely designed layouts.

- All rooms have good natural daylight and advanced air circulation systems.

- As exclusive caterers to the Reebok Stadium, Ring & Brymer, with a wealth of experience, are the foremost specialists in prestige events.

- Our accomplishments have excelled from catering for the monarchy, Ambassadors and dignitaries in days gone by, to today's pre-eminent service at Royal Ascot, Alfred McAlpine Stadium Huddersfield and Murrayfield Stadium Edinburgh.

- The standard of cuisine is exemplary - whether traditional or contemporary in style. Our unrivalled expertise, extending far beyond catering, ensures your event is managed with the utmost professionalism.

- The Reebok Stadium is located in a superb location, off junction 6 of the M61 motorway, and has 2000 free car parking spaces.

- Your event is as important to us, as it is to you and your company. Whatever your event, you can relax with the confidence that every detail in both the planning and delivery, will be second to none.

To discuss your individual requirements and bookings, simply call our Sales Manager at the Reebok Stadium.
Tel: **01204 673730**

Meetings

Conferences

Interviews

Training seminars

Exhibitions

Presentations

Weddings

Sportsman's Dinners

Company Dinners

Christmas Parties

Ring & Brymer
— GARDNER MERCHANT — .... At the Reebok Stadium

... one of the hallmarks of leisure at Gardner Merchant

Conference & Banqueting at the Reebok

Gary Atkinson
General Manager
Ring & Brymer

The Lion of Vienna Club

A presentation in progress, availability for up to 500 guests.

The Reebok Stadium, as well as being home to Bolton Wanderers Football Club on matchdays, on non-matchdays, it is a vibrant conference and banqueting centre, incorporating the largest purpose built suites in Bolton.

Its array of rooms, a total of 54, have all been designed and built to the highest specification. Their features include natural daylight, advanced air-circulation systems, generous ceiling heights, private bars, wide access doors and lift access. The two largest Suites, the Lion of Vienna and Platinum enjoy panoramic views of the pitch, as do the 46 Executive Boxes and Corner Boxes. State of the art projection, video and sound systems are added features of the Lion of Vienna Suite.

Each and every room can be easily adapted to create the right kind of atmosphere for each individual event - from a private dinner for 10, right up to a conference or banquet for 500 people.

The conference and banqueting rooms are situated in the West and Nat Lofthouse Stand within the Stadium. Both stands have large car parks adjacent to each entrance, reception areas and cloakrooms.

Level two of the West stand houses the second largest suite, the Platinum. Ideal for dinners for up to 350 people or a theatre style presentation for up to 500 people. With its added feature of the adjacent Piazza Bar, it is impressive in every way. This additional area is suitable for all different aspects of the event, from pre dinner drinks, teas and coffees, registration, exhibition displays and is adjacent to its own reception desk.

Adjacent to the Platinum Suite is the Sponsors Lounge. A smaller room but by no means less impressive. This room is ideal for the smaller, intimate affair of up to 50 people seated theatre or banquet style.

Level one in the West stand houses the Boardroom (Director's Guests' Room on match days) and the Wanderers Suite (Players Lounge on matchdays). The Wanderers is a very adaptable room, equally as suitable for a conference as it is for a celebration party. This Suite is self-contained with its own bar and toilet facilities.

The East stand is home of the Lion of Vienna Suite, as previously mentioned above. This suite, with its purpose built dance floor, can accommodate 450 for a dinner dance. State of the art projection, video and sound systems are added features of the Lion of Vienna Suite. Another Suite, the Burnden, due to be completed in August 1998, will accommodate up to 160 people for a dinner dance.

Ring & Brymer, one of the hallmarks of leisure at Gardner Merchant are exclusive caterers to the Reebok Stadium after being awarded a 10 year contract. They have a wealth of experience and are the foremost catering specialists in prestige events. Their accomplishments have excelled from catering for the monarchy, Ambassadors and dignitaries in days gone by, to today's pre-eminent service at Royal Ascot, Alfred McAlpine Stadium, Huddersfield, the Royal Albert Hall and Murrayfield Stadium Edinburgh to name but a few.

The standard of cuisine is exemplary - whether traditional or contemporary in style. Their unrivalled expertise, extending far beyond catering, ensures all events are managed with the utmost professionalism.

Since opening its doors on 1st September 1997, the Stadium has already played host to numerous prestigious events both the local and national markets, the North West Chambers of Commerce Annual Dinner, The 1997 National Training Awards Presentation and the Bolton and Bury Export Club Dinner.

One highly successful venture which brought together the three Stadium companies, the Football Club, Reebok Stadium and Ring & Brymer, was the hosting of The Antiques Roadshow for the BBC in November 1997 (due to be aired in March 1998). This took place in the Stadium's Exhibition Hall, which offers 35,000 sq. ft. of very easily accessible open space.

Events like these are fast assisting the Reebok Stadium in becoming recognised as one of the leading conference and banqueting centre in the North of England.

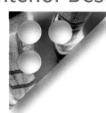

Interior Design - Charles Batchelor Sucha Design

Sucha Design were employed by Bolton Wanderers F.C. to be responsible for the interior design and interior contracting of the hospitality areas within the stadium.

The Board of Bolton Wanderers Football Club had taken up the challenge that the stadium was not for football alone, that the hospitality spaces created for football could and would be used 365 days of the year for functions, conventions, exhibitions, seminars etc. The competition for this business is great, mainly from Hotels, and even with the draw of such a magnificent structure, the Reebok Stadium would have to compete at the highest level.

The main thrust of Sucha Design is Hotels, Hospitality and Leisure - for the major Hotel groups. The spin off from this would be that the Bolton Wanderers fans would have some of the best interior designed facilities in football.

From the outset our concept was that the hospitality areas in both East and West stands should have a thread of continuity and continue the colour themes to the club concourse and open stadium and that the individual areas should be identifiable. The atmosphere should mirror the warmth and friendliness of the club. We believed that this could best be achieved through the flooring design.

Having researched carpets with club logos installed in many sporting premises, we came to the conclusion that none were practical or offered any comfort and warmth to the rooms nor did they do justice to the club's image. So it was that we designed the background carpet using the basic blue of Bolton and a palette of deep colours in a geometric design, in keeping with the Stadium. It is not a tartan, though many have laid claim to it with spurious Scottish ancestry suggestions being the McBain, Hargreaves or the McGinlay.

The basic design was then identified in each of the areas. The Platinum Suite, with the introduction of Platinum colours, the club logo interwoven with the new logo ribbons for a crisp mainly corporate image. The Lion of Vienna with the introduction of the rampant lion set in ribbons of gold and terracotta for a warm, lively function area. The Wanderers and Directors Lounge with the introduction of gold and green and a diamond motif taken from the furniture "in lay" for a cosy welcoming atmosphere as befits a Players Lounge and Directors watering hole.

With the base colourings of the carpets set, Sucha Design focused on the designs for the individual areas building up schemes of fabrics, wallcovering and paint finishes.

Lighting schemes and ceiling layouts were adapted to provide greater interest and options for the multi-function end use. It was also important to incorporate services that would be needed by the Function Conference or Exhibition organiser for visual and audio presentation, data and telecommunication and all within an attractive environment.

The last week leading to the first game saw long hours fitting the specialist blinds and blackout window treatments to satisfy the licensing laws for football; setting in position the 48 specially manufactured box tables; 1200 banquet chairs and tables; Sponsors Lounge sofas; poser tables and cafÈ chairs; the list goes on right down to selecting, framing and installing the pictures on the wall.

One area which gave us immense pleasure was the Chairmans Suite. He had commissioned the furniture for the room some eighteen months earlier and we were invited to view the furniture at the manufacturer's, Jim Greenall - a master craftsman. It is exquisite in traditional Georgian style with Bolton Wanderers' own pattern marquetry inlays. Our brief was to design the room around it and in keeping with it.

The entrance is through the mahogany doors where visiting Chairmen and dignitaries are shown through to the rotunda. This is the domed circular vestibule which is washed in blue light with spotlights picking out the Bolton Wanderers F.C. logo laid in the white and black marble floor. To the west, oversize mahogany doors curved to the wall lead through to the Chairman's Suite, to the east the doors to the pitch and the roar of the crowd.

As we were completing the Chairman's Suite, putting the finishing touches to the dried flowers, Graham Ball and Des McBain came in with top members of the board of Juventus, over to play Manchester United but taking the time to visit our own impressive stadium.

As I said at the beginning, working at the Reebok Stadium has been a joy and with still more areas to complete it continues to be a privilege to work on this magnificent Stadium.

The sight of the team training provided welcome respite and the opportunity to remember what was the most important aspect of the project. The whole thing has been about football and providing a community with a stadium in which to gather and appreciate the beautiful game.

As the stars all enjoyed their spell in our stadium I felt some self importance that I knew it better than any of them, but with it some sorrow that in two months notice it would no longer be ours and would be in the rightful hands of its rightful owners Bolton Wanderers Football Club.

As I saw many a ball hit the back of the net I stopped to consider the first goal at the Reebok Stadium.

Of course Alan Thompson thinks he has this honour, however the true identity of the first goal at the Reebok will remain a mystery that one day Arthur. C. Clarke may attempt to unravel. For now though, I will accredit Mr Thompson with the glory.

The summer sun continued during July and made for ideal site conditions. The progress was good if not a little hectic as we entered the period of the final countdown.

Abseiling and rock climbing techniques are employed in order to paint and maintain the huge steel roof framework.

The Middlebrook Exhibition Centre nears completion.

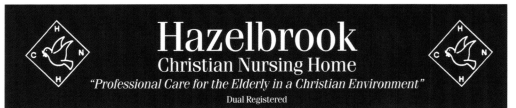

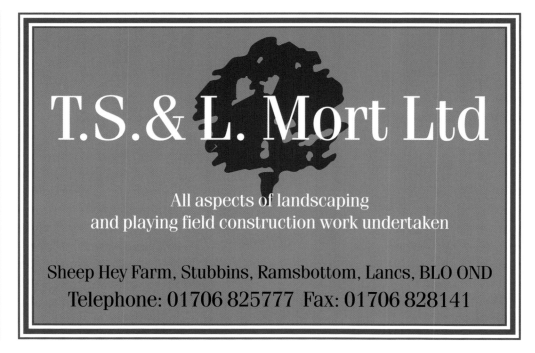

*Players Lounge
Wanderers Bar*

The Players' Lounge

Alan Fullelove
Press & PR Officer BWFC

It is the hottest ticket in town and getting hold of one is very much a case of who you know rather than what you know.

If the players' lounge were to be thrown open to supporters throughout the season, it would be an autograph hunter's paradise.

This is the room in which players from both teams meet up after the game with their friends and relatives. This is where they relax over a drink, discuss the match and get up to date with the news from the football circuit.

At the Reebok Stadium the lounge, appropriately called The Wanderers' Bar, holds around 100 people. But even a room as big as that fills up far too quickly and it's very definitely standing room only after any game.

Pre-match is when the lounge appears to turn itself into a creche. Wives and girlfriends, mothers and fathers, brothers and sisters, children and friends take over the room as the players themselves prepare for the action ahead.

Tea and coffee, sandwiches and biscuits are available from the buffet table while the bar staff are on hand to serve drinks, both soft and alcoholic.

For wives with very young children, it is possible to watch the game on Wanderers T.V. But for those who like the action live, it is a short walk from the lounge to the main stand.

For the players themselves The Wanderers Bar is an escape after the long round of post-match press interviews and a welcome addition to the Reebok Stadium facilities.

Director's Guest Lounge

Alongside the Wanderers' Bar (Players' Lounge) is the Directors' Guest Lounge. It is a place where guests of the Club from many aspects of the football world are entertained on matchdays. The Lounge can accommodate up to 150 people but normally a matchday will see around 80 people using the facility.

The bar has a particular feature. Cutting through the centre of the bar top is a 10" diameter bracing member used to give additional stability to the steelwork at this point of the building. Throughout most floors of the building these steel bracing members are hidden. As it cuts through the Directors' Guest Lounge interior designers Sucha Design made a feature of this particular piece of steelwork. As the bar is designed to resemble a ship the steel bracing member looks like a mast cutting into the ships deck.

The room is also ideal for small meetings, conferences, seminars and is used extensively throughout the week for these type of functions. But on matchdays the room has a particular atmosphere. Especially when Bolton Wanderers are celebrating a victory.

*Directors Guests Lounge
Photo: Ian Lawson*

Did you Know - Phil Hampson Resident Engineer

- There are 950 in-situ concrete piles and these are topped off with 438 pile caps of 52 differing types . . . each of the corner floodlights is held down with three arrangements of these pile caps . . . the smallest of these pile caps contains 230 cubic metres of concrete, and weighs 545 tonnes.

- The stand roof is approximately 27m (88 feet) high . . . the tops of the masts are 43m (140 feet) and the floodlights 56m (182 feet) above ground level.

- There are over 2,500 precast concrete units, all of which are supported by 3,100 tonnes of stadium steel, and further topped off with 1,650 tonnes of roof steelwork.

- The floodlights have a dual illumination: 800 lux to satisfy the requirements of the FA Premiership, and 1200 lux to meet the latest requirements of the UEFA/FIFA guidelines.

- Greater directional lighting is provided from the western side of the Stadium to aid television coverage and broadcasting.

- Over 24,000 square metres of metal decking was used to the upper floors . . . the total concreted area exceeds 40,000 square metres.

- There are two huge 500 kVA generators housed on the ground floor, and these feed the essential service boards, particularly used on matchdays and which consist of emergency lighting, emergency telephones, public address systems, turnstile counting, CCTV, and the like. Bolton Wanderers can produce electricity and sell back to the National Grid.

- The curved effect of the Stadium at roof level is held in place by the "dog-bone" trusses spanning the length of each stand and supported by the corner floodlight structures . . . each of these large trusses actually slopes inwards, the effect of which can only really be seen from outside.

- The blue roofing covers over 16,000 square metres and is of the Plannja type . . . below this to the rear, and at several differing levels, weatherproofing is provided by a flexible Trocal membrane roof approaching 5,000 square metres in area.

- Weatherproofing to the external facades is of several differing types: glazing, cladding, brickwork and blockwork . . . over 9,000 square metres of cladding has been used . . . blue engineering brickwork is a constant feature around the Stadium perimeter from Levels 0 to 1, . . . over 90,000 bricks have been used to this element alone, covering over 1,500 square metres.

- The white glazed blockwork used on the West and East Stands covers over 2,200 square metres and forms gigantic goal posts.

- 26,000 square metres of blockwork has been laid at Reebok, over a quarter of a million blocks . . . all construction at the lower level is of blockwork construction although, on upper levels, dri-lining was used to facilitate speedier construction and reduce drying out periods.

- 28 double and 4 single turnstiles have been installed to allow easier ingress into the Stadium by the public on matchdays . . . the same number of turnstiles could accommodate almost 40,000 people passing through per hour under the Green Guide.

- The Stadium has been designed on the basis of four separate buildings linked together, these being the North, South, East and West Stands.

- Each corner tunnel can accommodate road-going vehicles, and those at the south east and south west corners have been designed to be slightly higher to allow access for concert vehicles.

- Vertical access within the Stadium is provided via scissor stairs . . . mechanic vertical transportation is via lifts, some of which are of 13 person capacity to allow greater comfort . . . each lift is capable of taking wheelchair users . . . one in each of the East and West Stands allows stretchers to be accommodated.

- The piazza is approximately 15m wide and covers 10,000 square metres . . . it goes the complete way around the Stadium and gives pedestrian access to the visitors car park, the 'Banana' Road outside the West Stand, the Directors and disabled car park areas, the Club Shop and the Exhibition Hall.

Greater directional lighting is provided from the western side of the Stadium to aid television coverage and broadcasting.

Reebok Stadium 143

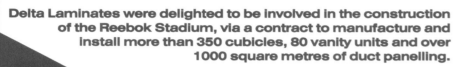

BWFC Merchandising at the Reebok

Chris Ball
Shop Manager
Reebok Stadium

Soccer merchandising is a huge business. Football Clubs, both Premier League and Nationwide League, are realising the potential of a well run professional retailing operation. The closure of Burnden Park, and with it the Club Shop, meant plans for a new retail outlet had to be devised for the Reebok Stadium.

It could be said that so long as an item of goods, whatever it may be, has a Club logo on it, that it will sell to a fan of that particular Club. This could well be true, but at Bolton Wanderers we had gone through the biggest change ever, and with the Stadium becoming one of the landmarks of design in English football, we had to continue the quality of design and thought, through into our merchandising and mail order.

Everyone by now is well aware that the main sponsor of the Football Club is Reebok. The team wear it on their shirts and the arena they perform in is the Reebok Stadium. It was an obvious benefit to us that the Club sponsor was one of the leading sportswear manufacturers in the world, therefore the expertise they had in retail merchandising, marketing, etc. would benefit our operation greatly.

We opened discussions with Reebok on our proposals for a new merchandising Store at the Stadium, with a potential for a second Store in the Town Centre. Reebok agreed to help us on the whole philosophy of the Stores, from the design and construction through to the operation.

As a Football Club, we were at the beginning of a huge learning curve. We had just moved into a Stadium, more reminiscent of a luxury hotel, with ten times the corporate guests we had known before. Just as with the hospitality, the merchandising operation had to be ten times larger than the previous one, and be able to compete within the sporting market place.

The location for the new Store was to be opposite the East Stand, towards the northern end of the Stadium. We had 5,000 sq. ft. of space which had to be designed to a maximum potential and have the look and feel of quality. With the help of Reebok's Design Team and our own Design Consultant, Andrew Hobson, we finally agreed on a scheme that would give us the results we were looking for. Display is of paramount importance. When units are busy, it is a major advantage for the customer to be able to see the product with the price displayed and make their choice before they get to the counter. This will therefore speed up the time of transaction.

*5000 sqft of floorspace provide stark contrast
to the old shop at Burnden Park.*

Excellent marketing exposure for both Reebok and the club.

Staff requirements are equally as important. Adequate toilet and changing facilities, along with hot water heaters for hot drinks and washing, are essential, especially when the Store opens for late night events. Staff are also dressed in easily identifiable uniforms so that visitors can easily distinguish official merchandise staff, and the corporate image is maintained.

The design of the shop has created a very upmarket image and provided excellent marketing exposure for both Reebok and the Football Club.

Once the plans had been agreed, the next task was to get the Store at the Stadium, and a second Store in the Town, open for the Christmas rush. Working drawings and building shop fitting work was done by ADP of Leicester. They had been responsible for many Reebok Stores in the past but, of more interest, had experience with the merchandising operation at Liverpool. F.C.

The Store at the Stadium opened on Tuesday 25th November 1997 with an official opening the following Thursday by the Mayor of Bolton, and the players. The Town Centre Store, situated at 12 Newport Street, opened a week later. In conjunction with the retail outlets, a mail order service is available, with a catalogue on request from the Stadium.

It is essential that Bolton Wanderers are able to compete with other Premier League teams both on and off the field. New retail facilities at the Reebok and in the town centre, now give us the potential to do just that.

A u g u s t

Finishing Touches

Dry run day'. Over 10,000 fans turned up on Saturday 31st August 1997 to view the stadium for the first time. The stadium was officially blessed by Canon Alan Wolstencroft, Vicar of Bolton.

With the beginning of August came the countdown to the project's completion. The twelve months preceeding this point became a distant memory and now was the time when the men would be separated from the boys.

The warm days had extended our working hours beyond belief and we were all grateful for the long days which enabled work to continue well into the night. Thoughts of holidays were distant and those of the staff retaining consciousness after the previous nights work managed to enjoy some of the late summer sun hovering over the almost complete stadium. The adrenalin that now pumped through the veins of staff and tradesmen alike served as the lifeblood of the project completion. Sixteen hour shifts were undertaken on a diet of coke and chips plus a substantial helping of camaradarie. On occasions the added incentive of a quick visit to The Bromilow or Barnstormers on the route home did provide an additional source of motivation and inspiration for some, not to mention me.

Days rolled into nights and with it the end date would loom ever nearer, there was no escaping it, it was tattooed on our brains. Members of staff would participate in a morning team meeting and would continue to encourage each other throughout the day.

As the level of expectancy increased, so too did the number of visitors to the Stadium, each of them eager to work out the location of their seats. Many would arrive late into the evening with the grim hopes of a guided tour or better still to see their team idols train, desperately clutching for scraps of anything to hold onto, just like we were for time.

The main reception nears completion

Gordon Hargreaves, Lofty and Nat Lofthouse lay the turf from Burnden Park, forever linking the old with the new.

The twelve months preceeding this point became a distant memory and now was the time when the men would be separated from the boys

The majority of hard work in a construction project is normally complete by the later stage, however, it is those final touches that make all the difference.

Consider having a room full of excited children waiting for the Christmas tree lights to come on only to discover the fuse has blown. This is the scenario of the final stage, it is knowing that once the doors are open, everything is going to work. Each of the fans will find his/her seat, they will all be able to buy food from the concession stands in quality surroundings.

The unique floodlight flag design which has a diamond framework carrying the lights themselves was soon picked up by the graphic designers advising the Stadium Marketing Department. This design is now used extensively for all Stadium signage.

As the end date neared, work continued right up until the very last available moment, our climatic, dramatic ending awaited us all.

For those there on opening match night they will remember the groundswell of expectancy that filled the Stadium and its piazza. For some this was just about football, whilst for others it was their just reward for many months of commitment and hard work.

For me personally it was the knitting of all these things together, for I love both my career in construction and my passion for football is only surpassed by the love I have for my baby daughter whose birth in May was the only milestone of the project which I have not mentioned.

Finishing off the roof paintwork to the Bolton Evening News Stand.

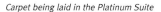

Carpet being laid in the Platinum Suite

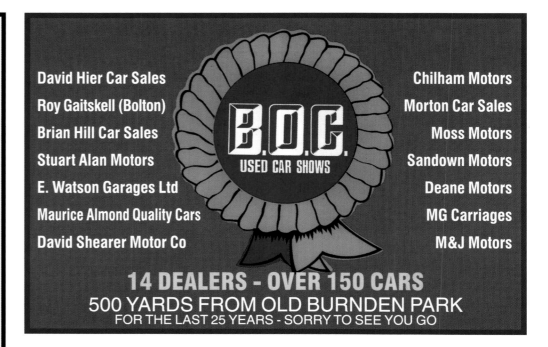

The Kick Off at The Reebok

Gordon Sharrock
Chief Football Writer
Bolton Evening News

The long-awaited first game at the Reebok was never going to match the hype and expectation that had built up to such a nerve-jangling crescendo!

Years in the planning, months in the building, 90 minutes of football could not possibly do justice to the work that had gone into such a magnificent new Stadium.

As events panned out, the Premiership contest between Wanderers and Everton was a disappointing anti-climax in purely football terms.

Of course, it will live in the memory forever. One of the true "I was there!" occasions to recount to your grandchildren in the years to come but it will not be remembered for the quality of football on show.

It had its moments and its controversy and Wanderers fans have argued long and hard about the "goal that got away" to back their claim that their team had the best chances to have won it. Had they emerged unscathed, the professionals would have considered it a satisfactory night's work but, sadly, the game that heralded the dawn of a new era had its darker side with record signing Robbie Elliott stretchered off after an hour with a badly broken leg - a personal tragedy for such a talented player on his home debut.

As fellow new arrival Peter Beardsley put it: "That's really of more concern than the result." The Elliott incident apart, Wanderers were relieved to take a point. They knew full well that things could have turned our much worse, resultwise, and recognised the fact that, performancewise, it was always going to be difficult to live up to such a glittering occasion.

They survived a torrid first quarter, frozen like rabbits caught in a blaze of headlights. Better teams than Everton would probably have punished them far more severely but Keith Branagen had just one serious save to make in the Bolton goal and slowly the tide turned with Neville Southall having to be at his best to save from Nathan Blake and Scott Sellars missing the target when he should have scored.

On the balance of play it was Wanderers fans whose spirits were highest as they sat back in their comfortable seats or queued at the modern kiosks and enjoyed their first 'interval' at the new ground.

Nine minutes into the second half came the decision that Wanderers will always be convinced robbed them of the win that would have graced the historic occasion.

Gerry Taggart had kept a vice-like grip on danger-man, Duncan Ferguson, and appeared to have crowned a magnificent performance when his header looped over Southall and dropped over the Everton line before full-back Terry Phelan hacked it away.

To everyone's amazement - and Wanderers had the Sky TV coverage of the game to support their case - referee Steve Lodge waved 'play-on'.

The Barnsley official's error (he later claimed to have been unsighted) sparked a debate that had every section of the football world considering the merits, or otherwise, of 'electronic eyes', 'fourth officials' and 'instant action replays'.

There was a deep sense of injustice in the Wanderers' camp - aggravated the more the incident was highlighted in the following days. But, despite everything that was said (Everton captain Gary Speed admitted the ball was definitely over the line) nothing could change events on the night and, apart from a good chance spurned by Blake, there wasn't another worthwhile scoring effort from either side.

For all that, the occasion was electric.

Many in the near-capacity crowd of 23,131 got their first glimpse of the spectacular new Stadium and the experience was a truly memorable one.

Had there been a goal for the Wanderers fans to cheer they would surely have raised the roof. Just five months after bidding an emotional 'farewell' to Burnden Park, they had settled into their new show home and were bursting with pride.

The emotional, pre-match minute's silence in tribute to Diana, Princess of Wales, who had been killed in a car crash in Paris the previous day.

The teams on that September night:

The goal that got away! Bolton v. Everton, opening match at the Reebok Stadium, 1st September 1997, final result Bolton Wanderers 0, Everton 0.

Wanderers: Branagan; Phillips, Bergsson, Taggart, Elliott (sub McAnespie); Pollock, Frandsen, Thompson, Sellars; Beardsley (sub McGinlay), Blake.

Everton: Southall; Thomas (sub Hinchcliffe), Watson (sub Short), Bilic, Phelan; Stuart, Speed, Williamson, Oster; Barmby (sub Branch), Ferguson.

Although there have only been around a dozen new Stadiums opened in the last 30 years, statistics show that the home team normally lose the first match as the occasion can often be bigger than the match for the home team players. So a draw under such circumstances must be regarded as satisfactory. What about the Reebok Stadium? A unanimous verdict . . . Magnificent!

SCAN

COMPUTERS

systems   **components**   **software**   **printers**

Scan International, 27-28 Enterprise Park, Middlebrook, Horwich, Bolton, Lancashire BL6 6PE
email sales@scan.co.uk web site www.scan.co.uk
Tel: 01204 474747 Fax: 01204 474787
(behind Reebok Stadium)

Shellnet

The North West's Premier Business Internet Provider
Varying levels of service for internet access & web site hosting

http://www.shellnet.co.uk

Shellnet Ltd. 2nd Floor, 12 - 14 Fletcher Street, Bolton, Lancs. BL3 6NF
Tel. (01204) 436709 Fax. (01204) 436711 email enquiries@shellnet.co.uk

Rock at the Reebok

Paul Fletcher
Chief Executive
Reebok Stadium

The design brief given to the architects was to ensure the Stadium was not only a football and leisure facility, but also a Rock Concert Venue.

Although the concept of staging a Rock Concert at a football Stadium appears straightforward, in practice it is far more complex. Most of the 91 league club football grounds are designed to get spectators in, and out, of seats. With Rock Concerts, the emphasis focuses on the need to get up to 20,000 spectators, safely, on and off the pitch.

As with football in the 1990's, Rock Events put spectator safety as the number one criteria. A licence must be obtained from the Local Authority who will normally use as reference The Guide to Health, Safety and Welfare at Pop Concerts (often referred to as The Purple Guide) for guidance.

This excellent document covers every aspect of the event including Event Management; Crowd Movement and Safety; Legal Duties; Seating Arrangements; Pass out Systems; Barriers and Fences; Staging; Mixing Towers and Sound Monitoring; Pitch Covering; Lighting; Access and Egress; Medical Provision; Facilities for People with Disabilities; The 'Pit'; Pyrotechnics; Parking; Signage; plus a multitude of similar considerations.

For football clubs staging Rock events, the 'crowd' profile provides a complete contrast to a normal football match.

There are some obvious differences. For example, a Rock concert crowd are all attending the event to see the artist, so in effect there are no opposing sections in the crowd, which removes the need for segregation.

The 'event day' is also far longer than the 2-3 hour football visit. In fact, many rock fans will arrive at the venue between 10 am - midday in the hope of getting a position in close proximity to the stage. For most spectators attending the event, their 'event day' is around 7 hours, therefore food, drink and toilet provisions obviously need careful planning. Especially where the profile of the Artist will attract a large female attendance and the need for 60% female toilets: 40% male toilets are required, in stark contrast to a normal football crowd which can sometimes be 6:1 male dominated.

An outdoor Sports Stadium event must not be confused with the indoor Arena event. It has been suggested in local press that the Reebok will be in direct competition with the Manchester Nynex Arena. Nothing could be farther from the truth. Where an indoor arena can stage events twelve months of the year because of the covered roof, a sports stadium is limited to the 3 months of June, July and August due to weather and football matches. On the positive side, where an arena can normally fit in around 12,000 to 15,000 spectators, a sports stadium can provide around 40,000.

Although the planning of an event such as a rock concert can take many months, the event itself takes around 5 days with the main areas being the erection of the stage and lighting plus the coverage of the pitch. There are various pitch covers to consider ranging from Teraplas to Tildernet to Portafloor. Often a combination of these floor covers provides the best result.

The effects of a Rock Event on the local community also needs careful consideration. A particular problem (often unfounded) is the 'noise' such an event creates. Many local inhabitants can be fearful that the sound generated by a Rock band will be heard within their homes, late into the evening. To safeguard local residents there are strict guidelines covered by Environmental Health which requires the promoter to employ independent sound monitoring specialists to: (a) check decibel levels at regular intervals during both the sound tests and the event itself, (b) react to any telephone complaints which arise.

Overall, the local community experience far more benefits from such an event than problems. On the event day 'Business is Booming'. As people travel in from all over the country, all hotels are full; restaurants booked up; garages, pubs and sweet shops report highest turnover figures. The secondary spend becomes a real boost to the local economy.

For the Town itself, becoming a Rock Concert Venue, brings both National and International acclaim. At the Reebok Stadium we are confident that it will not be long before Bolton stands alongside similar venues such as San Francisco, Rome, Paris, Sydney and Las Vegas.

Peter Myers
Director Touchline TV

Wanderers TV - Touchline TV

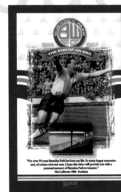

'The end of an era' video proved a great success amongst fans, showing footage that had never been seen before.

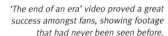

Touchline Television first joined forces with Bolton Wanderers during the 95/96 season. Initially the service consisted of providing match videos for sale in the Club Shop. These videos were filmed from the gantry at Burnden Park using a single camera. Commentary was added and the video was produced with opening titles before being duplicated and supplied to the Club Shop. Alongside these match videos Touchline TV also produced compilation videos again for sale exclusively through the Club Shop. These compilation videos contained highlights of the season so far and included information from behind-the-scenes, such as interviews with the players and playing staff. This service continued until half way through the Championship season of 96/97. It became clear that Bolton were on the verge of an historic season and therefore the video services were upgraded to match the performances on the pitch. All matches were filmed with 2 cameras both on the gantry, the pictures were mixed live and transmitted to the few TV's throughout Burnden Park.

The number of compilation videos also increased as Bolton swept aside team after team. The Championship season was comprehensively covered by 4 compilation volumes, a total of 5 videos. Bolton and Touchline TV produced a box set of all the compilations at the end of season as a collectors item covering the complete record breaking season. Two of the best selling match videos from that season were the wins against Spurs and Wolves both of which sold hundreds of copies.

During early 1996 Touchline TV was commissioned by Bolton to produce an historical documentary of the 102 years at Burnden. The result was a 90 minute programme entitled 'End of an Era - The Final Whistle'. The programme was hosted by Ken Wolstenholme MBE, a lifelong fan of Bolton Wanderers. As Ken is followed on his last tour of the ground we relive moments for the previous 102 years, including an interview with a man who was born in the same year as Burnden Park was opened. This much acclaimed video was complimented by an in-depth programme covering the final match against Charlton and includes the fans feelings as they watch Bolton play at Burnden for the last time. Both videos were supplied as a set and provide a lasting reminder of Burnden Park.

With Boltons move to the stunning new Reebok Stadium, once again the facilities provided by Touchline TV were improved to match the state of art stadium. Touchline TV created a digital control room within the stadium. This room is the heart of the match-day entertainment. Starting approximately $1\frac{1}{2}$ hours before kick-off the Wanderers TV station goes 'on-air'. A TV magazine programme is then broadcast to 150+ TV's throughout the stadium. This programme is produced 12 hours before kick-off to ensure it includes ALL the up-to-date news from behind-the-scenes. The programme includes interviews with the manager and players and includes highlights from previous games, both home and away. Approximately 1/2 an hour before kick-off the large screen within the stadium is also used to show the magazine programme. The technology supporting the large screen is incredible. Four powerful computers are used exclusively to control the screen, providing instant replays and team information. As kick-off approaches, the five permanent cameras which film the match come to life.

The match is filmed from 2 cameras on the gantry (one of the highest in the league) 1 at the side of the dug-out, 1 at high level behind the south goal and one at pitch level behind the North goal. Each cameraman is in communication with the match Director in the control room.

The Director instructs each cameraman what to film and views their pictures on an array of monitors. The 2 cameras behind the goals are used exclusively for replays to provide different angles on the action as the match is filmed, the pictures are mixed live and commentary is added live. The commentator also has a monitor so he can comment on the replays. The match is broadcast to all the stadium TV's and interesting replays are shown on the large screen. These replays can only be shown when the ball is out of play. Two master videos are produced during the match, one is sent to BBC and BskyB and the other is used to produce match videos for sale in the Club Shops.

The Wanderers TV station is one of the most advanced in the league and places Bolton in an ideal position to take advantage of future developments in the area of football TV coverage.

Sponsorship and advertising opportunities are available on both Wanderers TV and the large Videoscreen to companies wishing to take advantage of these powerful promotional mediums.

Photo: Ian Lawson
Instant replays are shown on the large 7m x 5m video screen.

Tours at the Reebok

Tom Hall
Visitor Centre Manager
BWFC

The Visitor Centre

From the day the Visitors Centre opened in December 1996 fans have flocked to the Reebok. Unfortunately, it wasn't possible during the construction period to let anyone into the building area for safety reasons but now that the Stadium is completed and fully operational many individuals and organisations are keen to look around the new Stadium.

The dressing rooms and run-out tunnels are always particular favourites. New facilities for the 1990's often raise an eyebrow such as 'kick about areas built within the dressing rooms', 'female officials changing room', drugs testing room'.

Tours are available most days except matchdays. Minimum numbers in a party are 10 people, maximum 50. Individuals or smaller groups can join other parties to make up numbers providing the time the tour has been booked by the larger party is convenient to them.

Stadium tours start from the Club Shop. During 1998 it is hoped to complete the new Visitor Centre, which will become the focal point and home for the Stadium tours.

If you wish to book a tour of the Stadium please contact the Club Shop (Tel: 01204 673650).

The Football Trust

One point of interest whilst on the tour of the Stadium is the brass plaque acknowledging the involvement of the Football Trust. The Football Trust has been providing support for the game at every level throughout the UK for over 23 years, and since 1988 has been helping clubs implement the recommendations of the Taylor Report. The governments commitment to the Football Trust has the support of everyone who cares about the National game. The Trust hand out around £40 million each year to help football clubs re-develop their existing ground or relocate to a new site. A grant of over £3 million from the Football Trust became a vital ingredient to ensure the Reebok Stadiums achievability.

The photograph shows Chairman, Gordon Hargreaves with Labour M.P. and Bolton Wanderers fan Ann Taylor leader of the House of Commonsand Deputy Chairman of the Football Trust, Richard Faulkner.

The Official Opening Ceremony

Another point of interest is the brass plaque in main reception. The Reebok Stadium officially opened on 10th January 1998 by the Deputy Prime Minister, the Right Honourable John Prescott, prior to the Premier League game against Southampton. Mr Prescott was welcomed to the Stadium by Wanderers' President, Nat Lofthouse OBE, Club Chairman Gordon Hargreaves and Chief Executive Des McBain before being invited to unveil a commemorative plaque in the ground floor reception area.

He then joined invited guests and civic dignitaries in the Chairman's Suite for lunch where he responded to a vote of thanks proposed by Club Director Graham Ball.

Immediately before kick off, Mr Prescott acknowledged the reception from 23,333 fans as he was introduced to both teams and the match officials.

The picture above shows the welcoming party applauding Mr Prescott following the official unveiling.

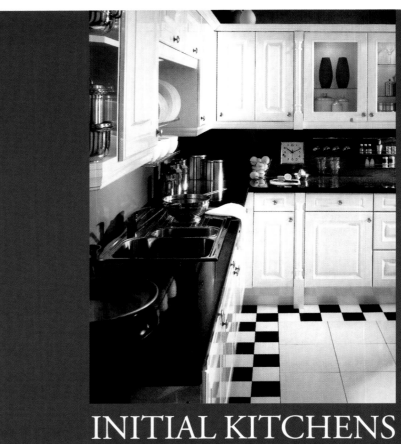